# WALKING
# CLASS
# HEROES

Tom Stephenson (3rd from right) on his famous Pennine Way walk in 1948,
with present and future cabinet ministers including Hugh Dalton (2nd from
right) and Barbara Castle (extreme left)

# WALKING CLASS HEROES

## PIONEERS OF THE RIGHT TO ROAM

### ROLY SMITH

Signal Books
Oxford

First published in 2020 by
Signal Books Limited
36 Minster Road
Oxford OX4 1LY
www.signalbooks.co.uk

A catalogue record for this book is available from the British Library

ISBN 978-1-909930-90-2 Paper

Cover Design: Tora Kelly
Typesetting: Tora Kelly
Front Cover Image: The view from near Kinder Downfall, Kinder Scout (Richard Bowden/Shutterstock)
Printed in the UK by Page Bros Group

# Contents

# Foreword by Stuart Maconie
## A hard won freedom

THERE ARE PEOPLE WHO THINK walking, or rambling as that rather quaint term has it, is a correspondingly quaint and genteel pursuit. They picture, one imagines, a man in tweeds leaning on a stile watching, as his briar pipe smoulders, a cow ruminating in the gentle Cotswolds dusk. Such people have probably never dithered on Crib Goch or Sharp Edge or slogged across Rannoch Moor or Eskdale Moss in a howling blizzard.

Even those rolling shires of Middle England though, that Gloucestershire field where the cow ruminates and the rambler enjoys his contemplative pipe, are steeped in a history of dissent, campaigning, activism and struggle.

The story of what we might call the "Outdoor Movement" in Britain is as much about that history as it is the (undoubtedly) valuable and much-loved joys of relaxation and exercise. We walk for many reasons, to taste fresh air, meet new people, enjoy new vistas and sensations, or just to feel the simple pleasure of freely putting one foot in front of another.

But that freedom has been hard won. In my role as President of The Ramblers, I am always at pains to point out that the roots of our movement are not in wandering lonely as a cloud but in the collective endeavours of people together, beginning with the young lads and girls of the industrial North who set out that spring morning in 1932 to walk on Kinder Scout in defiance of gamekeeper, landowner and the law.

Stuart Maconie,
President of The Ramblers

## WALKING CLASS HEROES

We enjoy the British countryside because of the ongoing efforts of the people celebrated in this terrific book; from poets to factory workers, from famous pioneers like Octavia Hill and GHB Ward, to legends like Benny Rothman and modern heroes of our movement like Rodney Legg and Kate Ashbrook. I hope you enjoy reading their stories as much as I did.

# Introduction
## Forgive Us Our Trespassers

*He called me a louse and said "Think of the grouse."*
*Well I thought and I just couldn't see*
*Why old Kinder Scout and the moors round about*
*Couldn't take both the poor grouse and me.*
*He said, "All this land is my master's."*
*At that I stood shaking my head.*
*No man has the right to own mountains*
*Any more than the deep ocean bed.*

This verse describing an encounter with an irate gamekeeper on Kinder Scout is from Ewan MacColl's famous 1932 trespass anthem, "The Manchester Rambler". It sums up the sense of injustice felt by many walkers before the advent of the Countryside and Rights of Way (CRoW) Act, which passed into law exactly twenty years ago. MacColl – then known by his birth name of Jimmy Miller – had been on the celebrated Mass Trespass on Kinder Scout in the Peak District that year, after which five ramblers had been imprisoned for daring to trespass on the then-forbidden moorland.

The Mass Trespass, which was opposed by the official Ramblers' Federations at the time, was perhaps the most iconic event in the century-old battle to regain access to our open country, mountains and moorlands, although there had been previous mass trespasses such as at Winter Hill in Lancashire in 1896. In this book, I profile twenty of the wilderness warriors – many of whom I was privileged to know personally – who fought long and hard to achieve our still-incomplete access to the countryside. Without these pioneering campaigners, modern ramblers would not have the cherished right to roam in open country which they enjoy today. Many of the featured characters were also ardent campaigners for National Parks in Britain, and next year (2021) will mark the seventieth anniversary of the creation of the first of these, in the Peak District.

1

## WALKING CLASS HEROES

This book describes the life and work of some of these campaigners and the battles they fought against seemingly intractable politicians and the Establishment, and it includes memories of personal encounters by the author with many of them. I have walked the Mass Trespass route with its leader Benny Rothman and his wife Lily, and part of the Pennine Way with its creator, my personal hero and mentor, Tom Stephenson. And I was proud to be a member of SCAM – the Sheffield Campaign for Access to Moorland – the group of determined trespassers who did as much as any to regain our right to roam in open countryside, and for the past several years have helped organise the annual Spirit of Kinder event in celebration of the Mass Trespass of 1932.

Readers might wonder why some other prominent names in the world of walking are not included here. The twenty subjects are very much a personal choice of the author, selected for the pioneering work they have done on access, and to give both a good gender and geographical spread. Prominent figures such as Alfred Wainwright and Walter Poucher, authors of some of the most popular walking guidebooks of the twentieth century, are not included because they never publicly took a stand about access.

Neither did the man who first came up with the idea of National Parks, the Lake District Romantic poet William Wordsworth, who called for "a sort of national property, in which every man has a right and interest who has an eye to perceive and a heart to enjoy" in his *Guide Through the District of the Lakes* of 1810. But Wordsworth later backed down from this noble and inclusive sentiment when he expressed his fear that the landscape of his beloved Lakes would be destroyed if "artisans, labourers and the humbler class of shopkeepers" were allowed to invade his precious fells.

Others who did campaign for greater access and who could easily have been featured include Canon Hardwicke Rawnsley, with Octavia Hill a founder of the National Trust and an ardent access campaigner in the Lake District; national Ramblers' secretaries Chris Hall and Alan Mattingley; folk singer and broadcaster Mike Harding, a close friend of both Benny Rothman and Tom Stephenson; and Patrick (Paddy) Monkhouse, Manchester journalist and author.

Monkhouse wrote one of my favourite walking books on the Peak, *On Foot in the Peak* (Alexander Maclehose, 1932), which actually gives the walker advice on where to look out for a gun-toting gamekeeper on an outlier of Kinder Scout!

> There is a faint path, but no right of way, and on populous Sundays a gamekeeper may be seen sitting with a dog and a gun on the side of South Head. His presence is usually an adequate deterrent, and the gun has not yet been used.

Many of those early access campaigners are, of course, no longer with us, but several others featured here are continuing the fight for the same kind of public access to the British countryside currently enjoyed by our neighbours in Scotland and the rest of Europe.

\*

Before the coming of the iniquitous Enclosure Acts of the eighteenth and nineteenth centuries, most of our open country, mountains and moorland was common land, where anyone could graze their sheep, cut heather or peat – or simply walk and enjoy the view. It had been this way for centuries, until it was stolen from the people by the landowning, grouse-shooting fraternity, who guarded it with falsely-worded warning signs and stick-wielding gamekeepers, determined to keep ramblers off their masters' land, such as the one featured in MacColl's song.

Nowhere was this wholesale land larceny felt more strongly than in the Peak District where, even as late as the 1930s, only twelve footpaths more than two miles in length crossed 215 square miles of Dark Peak moorland.

An 1880 booklet published by the Hayfield and Kinder Scout Ancient Footpaths Association claimed that the greater

Donald Urquhart, gamekeeper on the Inverewe estate
(Wikimedia Commons)

part of Kinder and its adjoining moors had until lately been known as "King's Land" – "over which the public might ramble at their pleasure." But by about 1830, the whole of this land had been allotted to various local landowners, "Trespassers will be Prosecuted" signs had appeared and aggressive gamekeepers enforced this legally-false premise.

The booklet described the situation:

> The award of acres may be thus tabulated:-
> To the rich, according to their riches      2,000 acres
> To the poor, according to their poverty      0 acres

No surprise then, that it was in the Peak District that the pressure for access to those forbidden moors, plainly visible from the back-to-back terraces, mills and foundries of people in the teeming industrial cities of Manchester and Sheffield, came to a head. On a sunny Sunday April morning in 1932, a group of about 400 of MacColl's "ramblers from Manchester way" deliberately trespassed on the forbidden ground of Kinder Scout, the bleak, moorland plateau which at 2,000 feet is the highest ground in the Peak District. After a brief scuffle with some gamekeepers, six were arrested and charged with public order offences and, shamefully, five were later convicted and imprisoned.

Benny Rothman, the twenty-year-old son of a Romanian immigrant, was the Young Communist leader of the trespass and as a result served four months in prison. The Kinder Scout Mass Trespass split the rambling movement and many, including Tom Stephenson, never approved of it. In fact, he said the best thing to come from it was MacColl's rallying song. An inveterate trespasser himself, Stephenson actually kept a dossier of assaults on ramblers by gamekeepers, and he told me that the main catalyst behind his invention of the Pennine Way, Britain's first and toughest long-distance trail, was an attempt to open up the forbidden Pennine moors to free public access.

The first to fulminate against the imposition of the Enclosure Acts was the Northamptonshire "Peasant Poet" John Clare, who saw the countryside he loved around his home village of Helpston gradually hedged and fenced off by the landowners whom he labelled "little tyrants" and "rude philistines". But Clare had a troubled mind, perhaps brought on by his frustration at what was happening, and he ended up in the Northampton General Lunatic Asylum, where he died in 1864.

On the other side of the Atlantic, that year also saw the creation of the first state-protected area in the world when, even as the Civil War was still raging, President Abraham Lincoln ceded the Yosemite Valley to California as a state park "for public use, resort and recreation". Yosemite will always be associated with John Muir, the Scots emigrant who was to become known as the Father of American National Parks. At the time, Muir was still working on his father's farm in Wisconsin, and it was not until 1868 that he eventually found his way to Yosemite and began his lifetime's work on its protection and the creation of other American parks.

At about the same time, Octavia Hill was working among the poorer classes in London, recognising the need for them to receive the health-giving benefits of the open air. Eventually she became one of the founders of the National Trust for Places of Historic Interest or Natural Beauty, with the aim that green spaces could "be kept for the enjoyment, refreshment, and rest of those who have no country house".

North of the Border another philanthropist, Percy Unna, bequeathed large areas of the Scottish Highlands into the care of the National Trust for Scotland, founded in 1932, subject to a strict set of rules regarding access and improvement – which have not always been followed. Unna's principles were continued in later years by his great advocate, Stirling's Rennie McOwan, which eventual resulted in the Scottish Land Reform Act of 2003.

There had been many abortive Parliamentary attempts to win back the cherished *de facto* freedom to roam such as that enjoyed in Scotland. These ranged from the first Bill promoted by Liberal MP James Bryce in 1884, to Arthur Creech Jones' inaccurately named Access to the Mountains Act of 1939. Far from increasing access to mountains and moorland, the 1939 Act actually limited access and introduced the possibility of making it a criminal offence. The Ramblers' Association declared that it "gave no access to a yard of land," and John Dower, the architect of England and Wales' National Parks stated in his famous 1945 report recommending their creation: "No access rights whatever are secured by the Act."

Inadequate provisions for site-by-site access agreements (mostly in the battlegrounds of the 1930s in the Peak District) were made in the 1949 National Parks and Access to the Countryside Act, but in reality only the Peak District National Park took advantage of these in any significant way.

Dower, in his seminal 1945 National Parks report, had recommended that access and facilities for public open-air enjoyment should be amply provided, picking out the Peak District, scene of the access battles of the 1930s, as the most urgent and pressing example.

Gerald and Ethel Haythornwaite, leading lights of the Sheffield branch of the Council (now Campaign) for the Protection of Rural England, had walked and outlined the boundaries of the proposed Peak District National Park long before. Ardent campaigners like Sylvia Sayer had performed the same function for the great southern wilderness of Dartmoor, which joined the Peak as one of the first National Parks in 1951, and Kate Ashbrook and John Bainbridge have continued in her formidable footsteps.

In 1985, the Ramblers launched Forbidden Britain Day, highlighting non-access moorland with well-publicised rallies. By 1991, this annual event had organised demonstrations on a scale not seen since the 1930s, and active pressure groups such as Terry Howard's Sheffield Campaign for Access to Moorland (SCAM) continued the campaign. Campaigning continued, with activists like Rodney Legg in Dorset and Colin Speakman in the Yorkshire Dales leading the claims for greater public access to the large areas of the British countryside from which walkers were still strictly forbidden.

Meanwhile, several Private Members' and Ten-Minute Rule Bills urged successive governments to take action on the long-promised legislation for the right to roam. When eventually a sympathetic Labour government was elected in 1997, the Ramblers were primed and ready for action. Supportive pledges had come from candidates of all parties before the election, confirming that they would back the right to roam, and the promise was included in the Labour Party manifesto.

Current Ramblers' chair and general secretary of the Open Spaces Society Kate Ashbrook was chair of the Ramblers' access committee, which was vitally concerned with the drafting and promoting of the CRoW freedom-to-roam legislation. Ashbrook was also active in seeing the Bill through Parliament, and she followed all the debates in both Houses and in committee, promoting amendments and providing briefings.

In 1998, Environment Minister Michael Meacher confirmed the intention to introduce legislation in a speech to the House of Commons, adding that it would be a lasting tribute to the memory of former Labour leader and keen Munroist John Smith. After some procrastination in the House of Lords, the resulting CRoW Act finally became law on 30 November 2000.

Although he admitted he was no rambler himself, Meacher said he saw the 1932 trespass as "a potent expression of the desire of those in nearby towns to escape poor and cramped living conditions for a few hours now and again, to enjoy the fresh air and wildness of the open moor." He told the seventieth anniversary gathering commemorating the Trespass in April, 2002 that he saw little need for confrontation: "not just because people will be exercising a statutory right, but because the new legislation also recognises the need of those who manage the land on which others will walk." Adopting a New Labour theme, Meacher added: "Walkers will have rights, but also responsibilities – to respect the countryside and its wildlife and the needs of those who depend on it for their income."

Before the implementation of CRoW, many landowners, including moorland owners and the Country Land and Business

Pendle Hill, in the Forest of Bowland, Lancashire
(PhilMacDPhoto/Shutterstock)

Association (CLA), had expressed fears of a rise in rural crime, disturbance of wildlife and moorland fires, all of which have proved groundless. Perhaps the most positive development to have emerged from CRoW is the fact that owners and users are now talking to one another through Local Access Forums, on which all interests are represented. Since CRoW, places formerly forbidden to walkers, such as the Duke of Westminster's Forest of Bowland in Lancashire, Butser Hill in Hampshire and the Brontë Moors of West Yorkshire, are now freely accessible.

The Ramblers' "One Coast for All" campaign contributed to the passage of the Marine and Coastal Access Act of 2009, which called on government to create a 2,800-mile path around the entire coast of England by 2020. The first section of the England Coastal path opened at Weymouth in June 2012, and work on extending the path continues, but it is still a long way short of that ambitious target. In 2011, the Ramblers launched the "Branch Out" campaign in opposition to the Forestry Commission's plans to sell off publicly accessible woodlands in England. The campaign persuaded government to rethink these plans and it continues to advocate increased access to woodlands.

The latest threat to access to the countryside is that all rights of way must be identified before a government deadline of 2026, after which it will no longer be possible to add old paths to the official record. The Ramblers' response has been to urge walkers to help in identifying an estimated 10,000 miles of historic footpaths that are currently missing from maps in England and Wales, and could be lost for ever if not registered by the deadline.

The situation in Scotland, where *de facto* access to open country had always been allowed, was always slightly different. Following intense lobbying by Ramblers Scotland, led by former director Dave Morris, the Land Reform Act was introduced in 2003, which established a statutory right to be on land for recreational, educational and certain other purposes and also the right to cross land. These rights have to be exercised responsibly, as specified in the Scottish Outdoor Access Code, which celebrates its fifteenth anniversary in 2020 year. In a year which marks the twenty-fifth anniversary of Ramblers Scotland, there is also to be a review of open access in Scotland.

The Covid-19 pandemic of 2020 caused a nationwide lockdown of the country. Ironically, it seems to have encouraged more people to realise the vital importance of walking and being able to enjoy the countryside. More people have been taking local walks where they can, appreciating more than ever the physical and mental benefits that only walking can give.

Finally, perhaps a word is needed to explain the title of this book. It derives from John Lennon's 1970 song "Working Class Hero". In it the former Beatle appealed to his audience not to be restricted by upbringing and never to give up on aspirations and ambitions. It also seems an appropriate axiom for the people featured in this book:

*A Working Class Hero is something to be*
*If you want to be a hero, just follow me.*

## Milestones on the Road to Access

| | |
|---|---|
| 1217: | Charter of the Forest re-establishes rights of access to royal forests for freemen and commoners |
| 1235: | First enclosures sanctioned by Parliament |
| 1604-1914: | More than 5,000 individual Enclosure Acts passed, enclosing 6.8 million acres of once common land |
| 1824: | Association for the Protection of Ancient Footpaths in York founded |
| 1826: | Manchester Association for the Preservation of Ancient Footpaths founded |
| 1845: | Another General Enclosure Act allows appointment of Enclosure Commissioners who could enclose land without Parliamentary permission; |
| | Rights-of-Way Society formed |
| 1865: | Open Spaces Society formed |

| | |
|---|---|
| 1884: | James Bryce introduces first Access to Mountains (Scotland) Bill to Parliament<br>Forest Ramblers' Club formed to retain Epping Forest as an open space |
| 1888: | Bryce presents second Access to Mountain Bill |
| 1894: | Peak and Northern Counties Footpath Preservation Society formed in Manchester |
| 1896: | Mass trespass on Winter Hill, Lancashire |
| 1897: | Co-operative Holidays Association founded |
| 1898: | Bryce unsuccessful again with an Access to Mountains Bill |
| 1900: | Sheffield Clarion Ramblers founded by GHB Ward |
| 1931: | National Council of Ramblers' Federations established |
| 1932: | Mass Trespass on Kinder Scout, resulting in imprisonment of five ramblers |
| 1935: | National Ramblers' Association founded |
| 1938: | Access to Mountains Bill proposed by Arthur Creech Jones |
| 1939: | Access to Mountains Act, including controversial clause which made trespass a criminal offence, passed |
| 1945: | Dower Report published, proposing National Parks, National Trails and access agreements |
| 1949: | National Parks and Access to the Countryside Act passed |
| 1951: | First National Park, in the Peak District, designated. First access agreements negotiated |
| 1965: | Tom Stephenson's Pennine Way, Britain's first long-distance path, opens |
| 2000: | Countryside and Rights of Way (CRoW) Act passed, giving access to open country |
| 2003: | Land Reform (Scotland) Act gives the public the right of access to any land for recreational, educational and certain other purposes |
| 2009: | Marine and Coastal Access Act approves an England Coast Path, to be completed by 2020 |
| 2012: | Wales Coast Path opens |
| 2020: | Twentieth anniversary of CRoW Act<br>Covid-19 pandemic national lockdown |

# 1: The Peasant Poet
## John Clare (1793-1864)

IN HIS ADDRESS AT THE unveiling of the memorial stone to John Clare in Poets' Corner, Westminster Abbey in 1989, Ronald Blythe, author of *Akenfield* and president of the John Clare Society, claimed he was "England's most eloquent and exact indigenous voice".

Nearly 170 years before, the twenty-six-year-old Clare, on his first visit to London, had stood on the same spot reading the tombs' inscriptions and wondering what his own future might hold. Four years later he would be writing instructions for his own tomb and epitaph, which he wanted to read: "Here rest the hopes and ashes of John Clare."

A major reason for this state of despair in the mind of one of England's most successful and widely read nature poets was the introduction of the hated Enclosure Acts. This pernicious movement, which robbed the English public of most of their ancient rights to common land, was famously described by Clare as a "curse upon the land". By the end of the eighteenth and the beginning of the

John Clare 1821: an engraving by E. Scriven from a painting by William Hutton (National Galleries Scotland)

12

nineteenth centuries, vast tracts of what had been common land for use by anyone in a parish had been surveyed under 4,200 Acts of Parliament. An estimated seven million acres – that is equivalent to the combined areas of Derbyshire, Nottinghamshire, Northamptonshire, Buckinghamshire, Bedfordshire, Hertfordshire, Cambridgeshire, Essex, Norfolk and Suffolk, or 20 per cent of the land area of England – were then parcelled off to local well-to-do landowners. This huge area was enclosed into fields more suitable for intensive and profitable cultivation, creating the familiar patchwork quilt landscape we know and love today.

But as Clare lamented in his poem "Enclosure":

*There once were lanes in nature's freedom dropt,*
*There once were paths that every valley wound -*
*Enclosure came, and every path was stopt;*
*Each tyrant fixed his sign where paths were found,*
*To hint a trespass now who crossed the ground:*
*Justice is made to speak as they command;*
*The high road now must be each stinted bound:*
*Enclosure, thou'rt curse upon the land,*
*And tasteless was the wretch who thy existence planned.*

\*

John Clare was born 1793 in Helpston, a small village which was then part of Northamptonshire, but after the local government reorganisation of the 1970s now finds itself swallowed up by the city of Peterborough. Still somewhat unkindly known as the Peasant Poet, Clare was the son of a farm labourer, and still worked as a farm labourer as he began to make his career as a writer. He later became a potboy in the Bluebell Inn in Helpston where he fell in love with farmer's daughter Mary Joyce. But the romance was doomed because Mary's father disapproved. Subsequently, Clare served for a time as a gardener at Burghley House in Lincolnshire, the grand Elizabethan seat of the powerful Cecil family. He later enlisted in the Army, tried camp life by living with Romany gypsies, and worked as a lime burner in Rutland in 1817. He was married to milkmaid Martha ("Patty") Turner in Great Casterton's parish church in March 1820.

Many poor families like the Clares had little or no land of their own and were employed as farmworkers, relying on the use of common land for the cultivation of their crops or for grazing their livestock. Almost overnight, the Enclosure Acts had made them landless and destitute. And the work that came with the enclosure of the fields, such as the planting of hedgerows in the lowlands or the building of drystone walls in the uplands, was often only temporary in nature.

In the case of Helpston, the land around the village was divided into three large open fields – Lolham Bridge Field to the north; Heath Field to the west; and Woodcroft Field to the east – spreading out like a wheel with the village at its hub. There was woodland to the south, including Royce Wood and Oxey (or Oxeye) Wood, which were among the favourite haunts of the young Clare in his unfettered exploration of his childhood landscape. As his biographer Jonathan Bate explains: "In Clare's world, there was an intimate relationship between society and environment. The open field system fostered a sense of community: you could talk to the man working the next strip, you could see the shared ditches, you could tell the time of day by the movement of the common flock and herd from the village pound out to the heath and back."

Clare was still only sixteen when Parliament passed the first Act for the Enclosure of Helpston and neighbouring parishes. For centuries the village had been centred on the open field system, and the local names of the woods and heathlands punctuate Clare's prose and poetry. As he recalled in "The Mores":

> *Far spread the moory ground, a level scene*
> *Bespread with rush and one eternal green*
> *That never felt the rage of blundering plough*
> *Though centurys wreathed spring's blossoms on its brow,*

*Still meeting plains that stretched them far away*
*In uncheckt shadows of green, brown and grey.*
*Unbounded freedom ruled the wandering scene*
*Nor fence of ownership crept in between*
*To hide the prospect of the following eye -*
*Its only bondage was the circling sky.*
*One mighty flat undwarfed by bush and tree*
*Spread its faint shadow of immensity*
*And lost itself, which seemed to eke its bounds,*
*In the blue mist the horizon's edge surrounds.*

But after the Enclosures, the scene was irretrievably changed:

*- a hope that blossomed free*
*And hath been once, no more shall ever be;*
*Enclosure came and trampled on the grave*
*Of labour's rights and left the poor a slave.*

Footpaths were closed off, and the right to roam previously enjoyed by all was suspended:

*These paths are stopt – the rude philistine's thrall*
*Is laid upon them and destroyed them all*
*Each little tyrant with his little sign*
*Shows where man claims earth glows no more divine*
*But paths to freedom and to childhood dear*
*A board sticks up to notice 'no road here'*
*And on the tree with ivy overhung*
*The hated sign by vulgar taste is hung*
*As tho' the very birds should learn to know*
*When they go there they must no further go*
*Thus, with the poor, scared freedom bade goodbye*
*And much they feel it in the smothered sigh*
*And birds and trees and flowers without a name*
*All sighed when lawless law's enclosure came*
*And dreams of plunder in such rebel schemes*
*Have found too truly that they were but dreams.*

## WALKING CLASS HEROES

In "Remembrances", Clare described his sense of personal loss at the disappearance of the open fields, and even likened the Enclosure Movement to the recent memories of the rapacious European empire building of Napoleon Bonaparte:

> *By Langley Bush I roam, but the bush hath left its hill;*
> *On Cowper Hill I stray, 'tis a desert strange and chill;*
> *And spreading Lea Close Oak, ere decay had penned its will,*
> *To the axe of the spoiler and self-interest fell a prey;*
> *And Crossberry Way and old Round Oak's narrow lane*
> *With its hollow trees like pulpits, I shall never see again:*
> *Inclosure like a Buonaparte let not a thing remain,*
> *It levelled every bush and tree and levelled every hill*
> *And hung the moles for traitors – though the brook is running still*
> *It runs a naked brook, cold and chill.*

After the Enclosures, many country people flocked to the new industrial towns to find work, only to experience a different kind of destitution and to become the victims of the 1834 Poor Law legislation, ending up in the hated and degrading confines of the workhouse.

Clare's first collection of seventy poems, *Poems Descriptive of Rural Life and Scenery by John Clare, a Northamptonshire Peasant*, was jointly published by Taylor and Hessey of Fleet Street, London, and E. Drury of Stamford, Lincolnshire in January 1820. In his introduction, his publisher and editor John Taylor praised Clare's vernacular style and responsiveness to nature:

> He loves the fields, the flowers, 'the common air, the sun, the skies;' and therefore, he writes about them. He is happier in the presence of Nature than elsewhere. He looks as anxiously on her face as if she were a living friend, who he might lose; and hence he has learnt to notice every change in her countenance, and to delineate all the delicate varieties of her character.

And Taylor added: "Most of his poems were composed under the immediate impression of this feeling, in the fields, or on the road-sides."

The book's first edition of 1,000 copies was an instant success. It sold out within two months, and a second edition of 2,000 more were sold by the end of the year. A further reprint soon followed in 1821. But although the London critics had raved over *Poems Descriptive of Rural Life*, Clare's vernacular, dialect-infused poetry did not seem to be fully appreciated by the educated classes, and he never won the fame and fortune of his Scottish contemporary, Robert Burns (1759-96). During his lifetime, four collections of Clare's poetry were published, but the sales of the later ones never approached those of the first.

Maybe it was his uneducated "peasant" upbringing and his unashamed use of dialect words, but he was never invited to London by his publisher, nor did he ever receive the support of a wealthy benefactor. Taylor in fact deleted many of his dialect words (like "pooty" for snail, "lady-cow" for ladybird

John Clare's birthplace in Helpston (David Laws)

and "throstle" for one of his favourite birds, the song thrush) and also attempted to make his poems more conventionally grammatical. This incensed Clare, but he was powerless to do anything about it because, unlike many of his contemporaries, he had to rely on the patronage of his publisher.

Even back home in Helpston, he felt that he was not accepted among the people of his own class, who seemed to think he had ideas above his station. He wrote: "I live here among the ignorant like a lost man in fact like one whom the rest seems careless of having anything to do with – they hardly dare talk in my company for fear I should mention them in my writings and I find more pleasure in wandering the fields than in musing among my silent neighbours who are insensible to everything but toiling and talking of it and that to no purpose."

Trouble in the form of poverty, personal loss and lack of success seemed to follow Clare wherever he went, and it eventually affected his mental health. In 1837, his friends decided to send him to a private mental asylum at High Beach in Epping Forest, Essex, where he stayed for four years.

The fragile state of his mental health can be judged by the fact that during his time at High Beach, Clare apparently claimed credit for the writing of Shakespeare's plays and Lord Bryon's poetry. He told a newspaper reporter: "I'm John Clare now. I was Byron and Shakespeare formerly."

In 1841, Clare absconded from the High Beach asylum to walk the ninety miles across country back to Helpston, believing in his troubled mind that he was to meet his first love Mary Joyce there. Clare became convinced that he was married to her and to Martha as well, with children by both women. In actual fact, Mary had died three years earlier in a house fire. He remained at home in Northborough, near Helpston, for five months, but his mental health continued to deteriorate, and his wife Patty was eventually forced to call in medical help.

At Christmas 1841, Clare was committed to the Northampton General Lunatic Asylum, (now St Andrew's

Hospital) where he remained for the rest of his life. He died on 20 May 1864, at the age of seventy-one. In accordance with his wishes, his remains were returned to Helpston for burial in St Botolph's parish churchyard. His grave simply records him as "The Northamptonshire Peasant Poet", with no reference to his previously expressed wish about his own "hopes and ashes".

In his 2003 biography, Jonathan Bate described Clare as "the greatest labouring class poet that England has ever produced. No one has ever written more powerfully of nature, of a rural childhood, and of the alienated and unstable self."

# 2: Putting Our Trust in Octavia
## Octavia Hill (1838-1912)

*Our lives are overcrowded, over-excited, over-strained.*
*We all want quiet. We all want beauty. We all need space.*
*Unless we have it we cannot reach that sense of quiet in*
*which whispers of better things come to us gently.*
   - Octavia Hill

**ALTHOUGH SHE IS PERHAPS BEST** known as one of the founders of the National Trust, Octavia Hill was also a pioneering social reformer and ardent campaigner for open spaces, which she thought should be made accessible to all. Throughout her life she worked tirelessly to protect green open spaces, especially around London and later nationally with the nascent National Trust. And her belief in the importance of access to nature for the wellbeing of the urban poor and the need to stop the destruction of the natural landscape are just as relevant today as they were in Victorian England. Strongly influenced by the belief that good environments make better people, she built improved housing and campaigned to give ordinary people greater access to the countryside.

Hill was born in December 1838 at Wisbech, the "capital" of Fenland Cambridgeshire. She was the third daughter and one of nine children of banker-turned-corn merchant James Hill and his third wife, Caroline Southwood Smith. Her maternal grandfather, Dr Thomas Southwood Smith, was to have a huge influence on the young Octavia. He was one of the leading public health reformers of early Victorian Britain and dedicated his life to campaigning for better housing conditions and for the urban working classes.

Both of Hill's parents were also keen social reformers and followers of Robert Owen, the philanthropist and founder of utopian socialism at his cotton mills in New Lanark. They opened the Wisbech Infant School as "a service to the wretched poor" and encouraged its use as "a hall for the people" in the evenings, with lectures, dances and meetings of the Mental Improvement Society. Members contributed weekly to the United Advancement Society fund to buy land so that the poor could grow their own food.

The Hill family lived in an elegant eighteenth-century townhouse – now a Grade II* listed building and a museum and education centre dedicated to Octavia's work – on the South Brink at Wisbech. All this was to change when her father was declared bankrupt after his bank failed. James fell into a deep depression and subsequently abandoned his wife and children.

Hill's mother Caroline took charge of the family, moving them to Epping in Essex and later to Finchley on the then leafy northern edge of London. These were idyllic days for the young Octavia, spent mostly outdoors "leaping ditches and climbing trees" and making hay on Hampstead Heath. Apparently, some of her earliest recorded words were: "Mummy, I wish I could have a field so large I could run in it forever."

In 1851, the family moved into central London when Caroline took up a post to manage the Ladies' Guild, a Christian Socialist co-operative financed by Edward Neale, a nephew of politician William Wilberforce, a leader in the movement to abolish the slave trade. At the tender age of fourteen Octavia was put in charge of the Ragged School's workroom at the Guild. The poverty of the girls at the school was to have a profound effect on the young Hill. She organised midday meals for her workers, visited them when they were sick and also took them on nature study walks around the London commons. It was the first of many initiatives that Hill pioneered to improve the lives of those less fortunate than herself.

Largely through her mother's connections, Hill also came to know the pioneering Christian Socialist minister Frederick Denison Maurice, whom she regularly heard preaching at Lincoln's Inn Chapel. She also got to know the socialist critic and campaigning author Charles Kingsley, of *Water Babies* fame, and the radical thinker and art critic, John Ruskin. In particular, it was Ruskin who taught her that people had needs other than those of simple economics. For Ruskin, anyone lacking access to art, beauty, and nature was impoverished. He distilled his philosophy into the simple dictum: "There is no wealth but life."

Inspired by these ideas, Hill set out to improve working-class living conditions. Then in 1864, backed by Ruskin, Hill was able to put her ideas into practice. She began buying neglected and decaying properties in London, refurbishing them and transforming the lives of the tenants.

Most significantly, instead of the common 12 per cent return on investment that many landlords expected at the time, Hill settled for a more modest 5 per cent, ensuring some of the money was used to keep the buildings in good repair and to improve the community. The scheme was an immediate success and rapidly expanded so that by 1874, Hill had over 3,000 tenancies in and around London.

In 1877, with her sister Miranda she formed the Kyrle Society, with the aim of bringing beauty, nature, arts and music to everyone. John Kyrle (1637-1724) was a noted social philanthropist from Ross-on-Wye, Herefordshire. Inspired by Ruskin, Hill realised that one of the greatest burdens of the poor was "not just poverty but ugliness", and the Kyrle Society was set up "for the diffusion of beauty" and aimed to bring "beauty to the people".

At the same time, Hill also became convinced of the need for open spaces for the urban masses in and around the fast-expanding city: "…a few acres where the hill top enables the Londoner to rise above the smoke, to feel a refreshing air for a little time and to see the sun setting in coloured glory which abounds so in the Earth God made," as she put it. She firmly believed in "the life-enhancing virtues of pure earth, clean air and blue sky".

In 1883 she wrote:

> There is perhaps no need of the poor of London which more prominently forces itself on the notice of anyone working among them than that of space. … How can

it best be given? And what is it precisely which should be given? I think we want four things. Places to sit in, places to play in, places to stroll in, and places to spend a day in. The preservation of Wimbledon and Epping shows that the need is increasingly recognised. But a visit to Wimbledon, Epping, or Windsor means for the workman not only the cost of the journey but the loss of a whole day's wages; we want, besides, places where the long summer evenings or the Saturday afternoon may be enjoyed without effort or expense.

She campaigned to preserve public open spaces at places like Swiss Cottage Fields, Parliament Hill Fields, Vauxhall Park and Brockley's Hilly Fields. It was through her campaign to save Swiss Cottage Fields from development in 1875 – where she was apparently the first to coin the phrase "green belt" – that Hill met Sir Robert Hunter (1844-1913), the solicitor for the Commons Preservation Society.

In 1895, prompted partly by the success of the Kyrle Society, in collaboration with Hunter and Canon Hardwicke Rawnsley (1851-1920), Hill founded the National Trust for

Hilly Fields, South London, 1903

Places of Historic Interest or Natural Beauty (the National Trust). One of its primary aims was that green spaces could "be kept for the enjoyment, refreshment, and rest of those who have no country house".

Rawnsley was a committed access campaigner himself. Forty-two years before the celebrated Mass Trespass on Kinder Scout, he had helped to organise several trespasses to open up land closed to walkers, including on Latrigg, the southern outlier of Skiddaw above Keswick, which was attended by an estimated crowd of two thousand people. In 1883 Rawnsley became the vicar at the twelfth-century St Kentigern's Church at Crosthwaite, near Keswick. He became worried that local landowners had been refusing access and closing footpaths which had been used for generations, including the routes to Latrigg summit, Friars Crag, Castle Crag and Walla Crag.

Rawnsley revived the Keswick and District Footpath Preservation Association and on 1 October 1887, two thousand people gathered in Keswick. The demonstrators marched up Latrigg singing "Rule Britannia" as they went, attracting enough publicity that it was reported in the national press. Canon Rawnsley himself was actually absent from the event, and the trespass was led by Henry Irwin Jenkinson, who is also remembered for raising the money to buy Fitz Park for the town of Keswick. The campaign eventually led to a footpath leading to Latrigg being opened to the public. Rawnsley was also involved in campaigns to improve access to places like Fawe Park, Keswick and to the seventy-foot high Stock Ghyll Force waterfall at Ambleside.

\*

For the next seventeen years until her death in 1912 Hill continued to fight for the preservation of the countryside and campaigned for the preservation of footpaths to ensure right of access to the land. Through her efforts and generosity the National Trust acquired some of its earliest properties, and it now cares for over 600,000 acres of farmland, 780 miles of coastline and 500 historic properties, gardens and nature reserves, "for everyone, for ever". Some of the first properties bought by the Trust at Hill's initiative were in the Kentish Weald, including Toys Hill, where a terrace commands outstanding views across the Weald. At nearby Mariners Hill, a plaque records: "The preservation of Mariners Hill as an open space property was due to the efforts of Octavia Hill."

Like the rest of her family Hill was quite diminutive in stature and indifferent to fashion in her appearance. Her friend Henrietta Barnett wrote of her:

> She was small in stature with a long body and short legs. She did not dress, she only wore clothes, which were often unnecessarily unbecoming; she had soft and abundant hair and regular features, but the beauty of her face lay in brown and very luminous eyes, which quite unconsciously she lifted upwards as she spoke on any matter for which she cared. Her mouth was large and mobile, but not improved by laughter. Indeed, Miss Octavia was nicest when she was made passionate by her earnestness.

Many of Hill's views were controversial. For example, she was against a welfare state giving out free school meals, council housing and a universal old-age pension. She argued instead that private enterprise and charity could solve social inequality.

Octavia Housing continues to provide homes for thousands of people in inner-city London thanks to Hill's vision and the generous donations by supporters. Despite her increasing ill-health, personal unhappiness and a nervous breakdown, Hill's empire grew, taking in buildings across the capital. She trained and paid a group of women housing workers and became a major public figure and policy maker.

In 1877, she collapsed and had to take a break of several months from her work. The causes of her breakdown appeared to be overwork, her inability to delegate to others, the death of her close friend Jane Senior, and the failure of a brief engagement. But in 1884, the Hill family found an ideal companion for her in Harriet Yorke (1843-1930). Yorke took on much of the heavy load of everyday work that had contributed to Hill's collapse, and she remained her close friend and companion until her death.

Hill and Yorke eventually found peace and contentment with the building of a cottage called Larksfield at Crockham Hill near Edenbridge in Kent, with its magnificent views across the Kentish Weald. Here Hill could take a break from her all-consuming work in London, and it became the base for her campaigns to save open spaces and to protect the footpath network.

In 1888, she helped to persuade the Commons Preservation Society to add footpaths to its remit, making the remarkably prescient claim (in view of the current threat of non-registration of footpaths) that they were "one of the great common inheritances to which English citizens are born. Once lost, these paths can never be regained. Let us before it is too late unite to preserve them."

Hill died from cancer in August 1912 at her home in Marylebone, at the age of seventy-three.

The secretary of the National Trust, Sir Lawrence Chubb (1873-1948), wrote in 1930: "When the time comes for the historian to apportion the credit to those who have helped save the commons and footpaths of England for the enjoyment of the whole community, I have no doubt that he will attribute much of the success to the influence and self-sacrificing work of Octavia Hill."

Octavia Hill, 1898, by John Singer Sargent (Wikimedia Commons)

# 3: Patron Saint of the Parks
## John Muir (1838-1914)

ALTHOUGH STILL RELATIVELY UNKNOWN IN Britain, John Muir, the Scots-born pioneering environmentalist has more protected areas, public parks and schools named after him in California than any other person. The immigrant Scot was voted the greatest Californian in 1976, and you can't travel far in the Golden State without coming across his name and rugged, white-bearded profile, which even features on the state's quarter dollar coin.

But Muir, one of the world's earliest and most influential conservationists and dubbed the Patron Saint of National Parks, is still barely recognised in the UK. The John Muir Trust (www.johnmuirtrust.org), based in his native Scotland, nevertheless now does sterling work in acquiring and protecting wild land, and he is commemorated in a fascinating visitor centre in his modest townhouse birthplace in Dunbar, East Lothian, on the North Sea coast in south-east Scotland. Even so, most British people still don't have a clue to who this hugely influential figure was.

The soaring granite domes, spires and walls of Yosemite, described by Muir as "Nature's cathedral", were his spiritual home. The spectacular, mile-deep valley in the Sierra Nevada 140 miles east of San Francisco captivated Muir from the moment he first set foot in it in 1868, as a rather reluctant sheep herder. Predicting the modern problem of overgrazing in British hills, he memorably dubbed the sheep as "hoofed locusts".

From the moment he arrived in the region, he spent the rest of his life campaigning for its protection as a National Park, an ambition which was finally achieved in 1890. Although nominally not the first National Park in the world (that honour went to Yellowstone in 1872), Yosemite became the first state-protected area when a bill ceding it to the state of California "for public use, resort and recreation" was signed by President Abraham Lincoln as the Civil War raged in 1864.

\*

Muir was born in Dunbar in 1838, the son of an evangelical Presbyterian who migrated with the family to the Wisconsin frontier in 1849, and he never lost that soft, Lowland Scots burr. Later in life Muir recalled: "When I was a boy in Scotland I was fond of everything that was wild... I loved to wander in the fields to hear the birds sing, and along the shore to gaze and wonder at the shells and the seaweeds, eels and crabs in the pools when the tide was low; and best of all to watch the waves in awful storms thundering on the black headlands and craggy ruins of old Dunbar Castle."

Dunbar Castle, whose ruins still dominate the former fishing town, is still watched over by the shark's tooth of the Bass Rock, guarding the entrance to the Firth of Forth. The castle was originally a stronghold of the Anglian Kings of Bernicia, and later became the impregnable fortress of the Earls of Dunbar.

Muir had a difficult relationship with his father, nearly losing his life in an accident when forced to dig by hand a ninety-foot-deep well on their Wisconsin farm. The young Muir was almost overcome by marsh gas and was lucky to escape with his life.

After making his name in Wisconsin as a youthful inventor (and nearly losing the sight in one eye after an accident involving a circular saw), Muir followed his boyhood love of the countryside, and embarked on an incredible 1,000-mile journey on foot from Kentucky to the Gulf of Mexico in 1867. "I never tried to abandon creeds or code of civilisation," Muir wrote in the flyleaf of his journal, "they went away of their own accord, melting and evaporating noiselessly without any effort and without leaving any consciousness of loss." And as a declaration of his breaking free from the bonds that had shackled his childhood, he gave his address on the inside cover of that journal: "John Muir, Earth-planet, Universe."

As he recalls in *The Yosemite* (1914), when he arrived in bustling San Francisco in 1868, with the original intent of reaching Cuba and South America, he asked a passer-by for the nearest way out of town. "But where do you want to go?" the man enquired. "To any place that is wild," replied the young Muir.

He eventually found his Shangri-La in the Yosemite Valley, and spent the next decade among the rocks, trees and flowers which were to become his natural home. He landed a job as a shepherd for $30 per month, guiding a flock of 2,000 of those hated "hooved locusts" to the Tuolumne Meadows in the High Sierra above the valley. The bonus was that this gave him the opportunity to study the flora and fauna and sketch the outstanding mountain scenery of the Sierra. His experiences were later published in *My First Summer in the Sierra* (1911).

After his stint as a shepherd, Muir found regular work at a newly constructed sawmill owned by James Mason Hutchings alongside the present-day Lower Yosemite Fall trail in the valley. During the two years he worked at the mill, he built himself a $3 shack made of sugar pine logs over a stream near the falls, where, he said, tree frogs in an archway of ferns "made fine music in the night" as he slept in his hammock.

His exploration of the valley was marked by his stoical constitution – he often went out with just a crust of bread to eat and slept out tentless for nights on end under the sparkling Sierra skies – and by his extraordinary daring. His derring-do exploits included shuffling out on a three-inch-wide ledge towards the very lip of the 1,430-foot Upper Yosemite Falls on a moonlit night, just to get a closer view. "The effect was enchanting," he wrote, "… fine savage music sounding above, beneath, around me; while the moon… now darkly veiled or eclipsed by the rush of thick-headed comets, now flashing through openings between their tails. I was in fairyland between the dark wall and the wild throng of illumined waters…"

On another occasion he deliberately took a dizzying ride in the top of a Douglas fir in a fierce windstorm, just to savour the experience. "The slender tops fairly flapped and swished in the passionate torrent, bending and swirling backward and forward, round and round, tracing indescribable combinations of vertical and horizontal curves, while I clung with muscles firm braced, like a bobolink [an American songbird] on a reed." After the storm, described in Muir's *Mountains of California* (1894), he famously commented on the interconnectedness of Nature: "We all travel the Milky Way together, trees and men"; and, "When we try to pick out anything by itself, we find it hitched to everything else in the Universe."

Among his other Yosemite adventures were being thrown about on the valley floor during the great 1872 earthquake; surviving a "gloriously exciting" avalanche in a Yosemite side canyon; and actually charging a large grizzly bear – just so he could study how it moved.

Muir was also the first to conclusively prove that Yosemite had been carved out by the glaciers of the last Ice Age 15,000 years before. Until then, the accepted geological wisdom, propounded by people like Josiah Whitney, Head of the California Geological Survey, attributed the formation of the valley to an earthquake or rift fault.

Whitney attempted to discredit Muir by branding him as an amateur, but Louis Agassiz, one of the premier geologists of the day, agreed with Muir's ideas and lauded him as "the first man I have ever found who has any adequate conception of glacial action". In 1871, Muir discovered an active alpine glacier below Merced Peak in the High Sierra, which proved his point and helped his theory gain acceptance.

Today he even has a glacier named after him in the Glacier Bay National Park in Alaska. Muir travelled to the area in 1879 and 1880 and wrote about it, generating interest in the local environment and in its eventual preservation as a national monument in 1925 and as a National Park by President Jimmy Carter in 1978. His visits were described in his *Travels in Alaska*, published in 1915, the year after he died.

Perhaps Muir's most notable visitor when he lived in Yosemite was President Theodore "Teddy" Roosevelt, who took time out from his political duties for a three-night camping trip with him in

1903. This was arguably the defining moment when the concept of "America's best idea" of National Parks entered the collective psyche. Roosevelt became one of its strongest proponents, creating five new parks, including Yosemite, during his term of office (1901-1909). The presidential entourage had travelled with Muir by stagecoach into the park. Muir told Roosevelt about what he believed to be the state mismanagement of the valley and the rampant commercial exploitation of its natural resources. Even before they entered the park, he was able to convince Roosevelt that the best way to protect the valley was through federal control and management.

After entering the park and seeing the magnificent splendour of the valley, the president asked Muir to show him "the real Yosemite". Muir and Roosevelt set off with a couple of guides and camped in the Sierra back country. The couple talked late into the night and then slept in the open air at Glacier Point and were dusted by a fresh snowfall in the morning. It was a night Roosevelt would never forget. He later explained: "Lying out at night under those giant Sequoias was like lying in a temple built by no hand of man, a temple grander than any human architect could by any possibility build." Muir, too, cherished that influential backpacking trip. "Camping with the President was a remarkable experience," he wrote. "I fairly fell in love with him."

Roosevelt (left and Muir at Glacier Point, Yosemite in 1903 (Library of Congress)

## WALKING CLASS HEROES

Earlier, in 1871, Muir had also been visited by one of his personal heroes, the philosopher and essayist Ralph Waldo Emerson. Muir spent several days with Emerson, and Muir desperately wanted Emerson to camp with him in the Mariposa Grove of giant sequoias. But Emerson's travelling companions would not allow the aged essayist to do so. Muir wrote of Emerson: "Emerson was the most serene, majestic, Sequoia-like soul I ever met. His smile was as sweet and calm as morning light on mountains. There was a wonderful charm in his presence; his smile, serene eye, his voice, his manner, were all sensed at once by everybody. I felt here was a man I had been seeking."

According to Muir's friend John Swett, on his return from seeing Yosemite with Muir, Emerson said of Muir, "He is more wonderful than Thoreau," a reference to Henry David Thoreau (1817-1862), the writer and transcendentalist poet best known for his book, *Walden, Or Life in the Woods* (1854).

National Parks have often been described as "America's best idea", and John Muir as their father. It would take another seventy-nine years after the creation of Yellowstone in 1872 before this idea came to fruition in Britain, with the creation of the Peak District, Lake District, Snowdonia and Dartmoor parks in 1951.

Muir married Louisa (Louie) Wanda Strentzel in 1880 and ran the family's 2,600-acre fruit farm at Martinez in the Alhambra Valley, north of San Francisco, for five years, where they brought up their two daughters, Wanda and Helen. As I discovered in a pilgrimage to his Italianate-style house in 2003, it is now somewhat incongruously surrounded by powerlines and buzzing freeways.

But Muir was never a natural fruit-grower, and he constantly pined for his beloved mountains. He was encouraged by his lifelong friend and mentor Jeanne Carr to laboriously write up his memories in what he called his "scribble den" on the top floor of the house. He continued to campaign for the preservation of America's scenic heritage, founding the influential environmental pressure group, the Sierra Club, in 1892.

By far the greatest disappointment of Muir's life was that he failed to stop the flooding of the Hetch Hetchy Valley, north-east of Yosemite, by the O'Shaughnessy Dam to create a reservoir for the fast-expanding city of San Francisco in 1913. "Dam Hetch Hetchy!" he fumed in *The Yosemite*. "As well dam for water tanks the people's cathedrals and churches, for no holier temple has ever been consecrated by the heart of man." He died a year later in a San Francisco hospital of

John Muir, 1909 (Library of Congress, Washington DC

pneumonia – allegedly brought on by a broken heart over the loss of Hetch Hetchy.

The towering granite canyon and tumbling waterfalls of Yosemite will always remain Muir's lasting monument. Although in high summer the valley floor is thronged with tourists, crammed with shopping outlets, and blighted by a notorious one-way traffic system, if you follow Muir's advice you can still find that:

> … going to the mountains is going home; that wildness is a necessity; and mountain parks and reservations are useful not only as fountains of timber and irrigating rivers, but as fountains of life.

# 4: "The Man Who Never Was Lost Never Went Very Far"
## GHB Ward (1876-1957)

THE EXHORTATION BY **GHB "BERT"** Ward about the forthcoming Revellers' Ramble of the Sheffield Clarion Ramblers' Club for Sunday 10 January 1926 could not been clearer:

> We go wet or fine, snow or blow, and none but the bravest and fittest must attempt this walk. Those who are unwell, unfit, inexperienced or insufficiently clad, should consult their convenience, and ours, by staying at home. Ladies, on this occasion, are kindly requested not to attend.

Such was the typically authoritarian, not to say sexist, tone of Ward, so-called King of the Clarion Ramblers, who for half a century led one of the earliest and foremost rambling clubs in Britain, leaving behind a unique legacy of outdoor literature.

Almost single-handedly Ward produced the tiny Clarion Ramblers' Handbooks for over fifty years, and he was fond of inserting pithy (and equally sexist) aphorisms in them, such as: "The man who never was lost never went very far" and "A rambler made is a man improved." They also included quotations from literary giants such as William Wordsworth, John Ruskin, and from across the Atlantic, Henry David Thoreau, Ralph Waldo Emerson and Walt Whitman.

This was at a time when ordinary working-class members of his club did not always have access to such writers, except in public libraries. Rambling for Ward was, as he said himself, "the trinity of legs, eyes and mind", and through his treasured and widely read Handbooks he hoped to disseminate his particular brand of open-air socialism.

Clarion Ramblers Handbooks (Derbyshire Record Office)

George Herbert Bridges Ward was born in 1876 in Derwent Street, Sheffield, but ten months later his family moved to Glen Cottage, Park Farm, then on the edge of the smoky grime of the heavily industrialised Steel City.

He attended St John's National School until he was thirteen, when he won a scholarship to Sheffield's Central High School. But probably due to family circumstances (his mother had died when he was nine), he did not take it up. Instead he started work as an errand boy at a Sheffield silversmiths, but was sacked for refusing to work on a Saturday (probably because it interfered with his walking expeditions). He subsequently found another job at a stay busk manufacturing company, where he remained from 1891 to 1900, serving an apprenticeship until 1897, when he qualified as an engineer fitter.

The year 1900 was to prove highly significant in Ward's life. His father and his maternal grandfather both died, and he left the engineering company in 1900 and had a long holiday in the Canary Islands – hardly a typical holiday destination for a Sheffield fitter at the time. This experience sparked in Ward a life-long interest in Spain, which became the subject of his only published book, *The Truth about Spain* (1911), in which he accurately predicted the Spanish Civil War (1936-39) and its inevitable consequence in the form of the Second World War. He wrote: "If Rome, on her part, fails to read the signs of the times, then within a decade – a little less or a little more – a social conflagration will break out in Spain that will light the world."

On Sunday 2 September, 1900, Ward organised the first Sheffield Clarion ramble, a round of the then-forbidden 2,000-foot moorland plateau of Kinder Scout, the highest ground in the Peak District. Jack Jordan, one of the walkers, claimed after the twenty-mile walk: "… if our feet were on the heather, our hearts and hopes were with the stars."

That first Clarion ramble seems to have been based on an article in the *Sheffield Daily Independent* by editor John Derry (1854-1937). "The Round of Kinder", as the walk was dubbed, had been made possible from Sheffield by the opening to passengers of the railway line from Sheffield to Manchester via Hope and Edale in 1894, and, following long negotiations by the Peak and Northern Footpaths Society, by the re-opening of the public right of way from Hayfield to the Snake Inn via William Clough in 1897. Ward had apparently done a reconnaissance of the route, and he claimed to have advertised the ramble in Robert Blatchford's socialist newspaper, *The Clarion* – which gave the subsequent rambling club, the Sheffield Clarion Ramblers, its name.

Most, if not all, of the eleven men and three women who turned up on that sunny autumn morning would have, however, probably known each other already from the Saturday afternoon meetings of the Clarion Vocal Union in Sheffield. In the summer months, these included a walk and a sing-song in what would later become Sheffield's Green Belt.

The route taken by those original Clarions took them from Edale station up Jacob's Ladder to Edale Cross and by Coldwell

Clough and down into Hayfield for lunch. The group had lunch and "a good sing-song" at a pub in Hayfield and then went up the Kinder Road to Kinder Bank and William Clough (scene of the 1932 Mass Trespass) and down Ashop Clough, where the men even had time for a swim. Jordan recalled: "Now the descent of Ashop Clough was before us, and after persuading the ladies to go on ahead, several of the men indulged in a bathe in one of the deeper pools." Naturism, inspired by people like the Sheffield-based socialist Edward Carpenter and the American poet Walt Whitman, seems to have formed an important part of open-air socialism at the time. There is a famous photograph of Ward engaged in what would today be called "skinny-dipping" in a waterfall-fed pool near Swain's Greave close to Bleaklow's boggy summit.

GHB Ward skinny-dipping at Bleaklow (Ramblers)

Sheffield Clarion Ramblers at the Barrel Inn, Bretton after their 30th anniversary ramble in 1930. Ward (centre right) has his arms around a fellow member.

Tea was enjoyed at the Snake Inn, where the landlord, unused in those days to seeing such a large group of walkers, set to and baked them some fresh bread cakes. The total cost per head of this fine repast of bread cakes and boiled ham was the princely sum of 1s 3d (6p)! After tea, the group took the road down to Alport Bridge and then up to Hope Cross, finally descending to Hope station to catch the train home to Sheffield. Jordan noted at the end of the walk that Ward had kept repeating: "Pioneers, oh pioneers!" as if he knew on that day that they were forerunners of what was to become a great walking tradition in Sheffield.

The Round of Kinder became an annual anniversary ramble for the club, and the forbidden plateau itself – the Holy Grail for ramblers – soon also attracted members, despite the threatening presence of stick-wielding gamekeepers.

The following April, Ward married his wife Fanny Bertha, and the couple eventually had six children – four sons and two daughters – who survived infancy. From 1901 to 1912 Ward worked as a fitter at Kelham Island Power Station, and he was involved in trade union political work which initially gave him less time to devote to rambling. But rambling was always his first love, as is made clear by Ward's articles in the local radical newspaper, *The Sheffield Guardian*. In the edition of 21 June 1907, a correspondent complained that there were too many articles about country walks and cycle rides, and practically nothing about the Labour Representation Committee. Ward replied: "There's politics and there's fresh air"; and "some of us found our socialism not in the clangings and the hammerings" but in "the picture of the countryside… in the sketches of the ivied cottage, in the snatches of simple thought, in character and simplicity, in the socialism that never seemed more present than when perhaps most absent, or least intrusive."

In 1912, Ward started working for the Ministry of Labour, and the First World War took him to work in London at the Ministry of Munitions, where he became acquainted with Rudyard Kipling's "blunt, bow-headed whaleback" Sussex Downs. But he continued to write and edit the Clarion Handbooks and to join club rambles at weekends.

He returned to Sheffield in 1919, when he moved with his growing family to a house at Owler Bar on the Derbyshire outskirts of the city, where he lived until his death in 1957. After the war he continued his work in Sheffield as a Conciliation Officer until his retirement in 1941, when he was able to devote himself more fully to rambling and access to the countryside.

Although he is still sometimes erroneously described as one of the organisers, Ward played no part in the planning of the 1932 Kinder Scout Mass Trespass. As a civil servant, he knew his job would have been at risk, and he was a leading member of the official Ramblers' Federation, which had officially opposed the action.

Nonetheless Ward was no stranger to what he dubbed "the gentle art of trespass". He had been advocating it since long before 1932 and was served with a writ by moorland owner James Watts in 1923 forbidding him from walking on his land on the western side of Kinder Scout.

Ward not only founded the Clarion Ramblers but was also the founder or a founding member of several local organisations including the Sheffield Ramblers' Federation in 1926, part of the National Council of Ramblers' Federations which became the Ramblers' Association in 1935. He was also closely involved in the Hallamshire Footpath Preservation Society, the Hunter Archaeological Society and the Sheffield Society for the Protection of Scenery, which later became the Sheffield branch of CPRE and Friends of the Peak.

He refused an OBE in 1941 but was later happy to accept two local honours. In 1945, after some what would be called today "crowd-funding" in appreciation of his contribution to the outdoors, the 1,563-foot summit of Lose Hill Pike (now known as "Ward's Piece") was presented to him, and he immediately handed over the deeds to the National Trust. Another recognition of his services to the outdoors rather poignantly came on his deathbed at Nether Edge Hospital, Sheffield in 1957, when he was awarded an honorary MA degree from the University of Sheffield.

The South Yorkshire and North East Derbyshire Area of the Ramblers received a bequest from the Ward estate which allowed it to contribute towards the development of a moorland garden in Ward's honour at the National Trust's Moorland Discovery Centre at Longshaw Lodge, above Hathersage. This garden, named Ward's Croft, opened in 2009 and allows inner city children to learn about their moorland heritage.

Ward expert Dave Sissons, said: "Ward's contribution to rambling, access to moorlands and protection of the countryside was phenomenal. But his most lasting legacy must be the Clarion Handbooks. They are collectors' items and mines of local history and folklore, and an enduring record of the struggle for access to the countryside which preceded the CRoW Act." I am proud to be one of those avid collectors of Clarion Handbooks, and when I worked as Head of Information Services for the Peak District National Park authority, the archaeologists on the staff would often ask me for copies of a Handbook for a certain year. Ward's detailed research and encyclopaedic knowledge of the Peak, meticulously recorded in his detailed, hand-drawn maps of each walk, even noting individual field names, were wonderful sources of information about the past landscapes of the Park.

Terry Howard, a leading modern Sheffield access campaigner (see Chapter 13), is another long-time admirer. "I read my first Sheffield Clarion Handbook more than half a century ago. It was full of information about Lockerbrook Farm, a place where I loved to visit and where I spent a lot of time as a member of the Woodcraft Folk. I was hooked straight away and have been ever since on these little gems of outdoor literature.

"They also illustrate the life of a remarkable man who almost single-handedly wrote and edited the handbooks for 50 years, and was totally committed to enabling people to explore, understand and appreciate the local countryside," Howard said. "It is difficult to imagine the total commitment he must have had to research and produce these little treasures of information."

Howard adds that one of the most fascinating aspects of the Clarion Handbooks was how Ward had collected stories, anecdotes and memories, going back as far as the early years of the nineteenth century. Ward's meticulous research helped to shed light on many issues concerning rights of way and moorland access in disputed areas even up to the present day.

Ward himself explained this pioneering work in a lecture he gave on moorland bridle paths to the Hunter Archaeological Society in Sheffield in February 1921: "This lecture is the result of a manhood's leisure spent in rambling over lonely places and wild moorlands... I have followed no one and nobody's investigations for, if one could, there are remarkably few who have left any moorland records to copy or improve upon."

# 5: The Man who Bought Mountains
## Percy Unna (1878 – 1950)

IT WAS ONCE SAID OF the Scottish industrialist and philanthropist Percy Unna that he gave away a fortune to buy a wilderness.

Of Danish extraction but born in London, Unna was educated at Eton and Trinity College, Cambridge. He later became a wealthy and respected civil engineer. During the First World War he served in the Navy as a Lieutenant Commander on an auxiliary patrol vessel based in Leith and later serving in the Bristol Channel and Egypt. After the war, his experience as a civil engineer took him to West Africa for a time.

During the Second World War he helped construct the Mulberry Harbours which were used after D-Day in June 1944. Mulberry Harbours were temporary portable harbours developed to facilitate the rapid off-loading of cargo onto beaches during the Allied invasion of Normandy. After the beach heads had been successfully established, the prefabricated harbours were taken in sections across the English Channel and assembled off Omaha and Gold Beaches.

He was always keen to preserve his anonymity so not much is known about Unna, and he has been called the "mystery man" of the Scottish mountains. But he was a keen and accomplished mountaineer and became a member in 1904 and later president of the Scottish Mountaineering Club (SMC) in 1936. He was also an experienced Alpinist, with many difficult routes to his credit after several seasons spent in the Alps.

As climbing partner Dr NS Finzi recalled in the *Alpine Journal*: "Though he was a very small eater, he was extraordinarily resistant to cold. We always had the window wide open, and I shall never forget waking one morning when the thermometer was minus 15 deg C, to find him calmly sleeping with both bare feet projecting beyond the end of the blankets and almost out of the window. He would also stand about in a bitter cold wind taking photographs, when we others had to keep moving to get warm."

Unna was remembered in the SMC as an eccentric character with a mischievous, even puckish, sense of humour. A former secretary recalled as he attended an SMC meeting in 1945-46 hearing a voice welcoming him from the carpet of the smoke-filled room. It was Unna, who believed that an hour spent flat out on the floor after dinner stimulated the digestion – and probably also avoided the choking tobacco fumes.

An instance of Unna's innate kindliness occurred when he was staying at the Kintail Hotel and discovered that his field glasses had been stolen. He realised that the culprit was a tramp whom he'd just seen passing by, so Unna seized a bicycle and set off in pursuit. He caught up with the tramp, retrieved his glasses and then had a long talk with him about the need for him to mend his ways. Apparently, he found the man "an interesting character" and he took no further action against him. Unna also discovered that the London Transport by-laws did not include a regulation that passengers must produce their tickets when asked to do so by an inspector. He was said to have spent many happy hours travelling by bus hoping to be asked to show his ticket and then disputing with the inspector when asked to do so.

It was through his membership of the SMC that Unna met other climbers who were supporters and members of the National Trust for Scotland (NTS). He was to become deeply involved in the Trust's activities and particularly in its policy of allowing open access to its countryside properties.

From its very beginning, the NTS was committed to protecting Scotland's rich natural and man-made heritage. Sir John Stirling Maxwell, later to be NTS President, said at the Trust's first Annual General Meeting in 1932: "The National Trust for Scotland serves the nation as a cabinet into which it can put some of its valuable things, where they will be perfectly safe for all time, and where they are open to be seen and enjoyed by everyone."

It led to Unna's enthusiasm to protect the natural landscapes of Scotland and he set about raising funds to purchase much the Glencoe Estate of Lord Strathcona in 1935. This was followed by the Dalness Forest – including the magnificent mountains which guard the entrance to Glencoe – Buachaille Etive Mor and Buachaille Etive Beag – two years later. To ensure the continued upkeep of the estate, Unna made out a seven-year covenant to the Trust, amounting to over £20,000, which today would be worth over £1 million.

Buachaille Etive Mor,
at the entrance to Glencoe

The Dalness Estate was formally handed over to the NTS in 1937 by the SMC from the funds raised by Unna. In doing so he formulated what became known as the Unna Rules (see Box), which were intended to ensure the land was held on behalf of the public and preserved for their use in a "primitive" condition, without development or active management. These have given rise to subsequent controversy, such as accusations that the NTS has compromised the Unna Rules with, for example, the metal footbridge which crosses the River Coe and leads to Coire Gabhail ("the Lost Valley") above Glencoe.

As early as the 1930s, Unna was concerned about the appearance of unnecessary cairns on mountain paths, which he said were unsightly, caused erosion and were an unreliable navigational aid. With friends he formed an informal club with the Biblical name of "the Gadarene Swine", whose aim was to demolish as many of these cairns as they could. I remember watching approvingly as the then NTS Chief Ranger Paul Johnson did just that as we took the path from the Trust's Mar Lodge estate towards the Lairig Ghru and the Corrour Bothy beneath The Devil's Point back in the 1990s.

For the remainder of his life Unna made considerable anonymous donations to the Trust to ensure the upkeep of these estates and to enable the purchase of further wilderness areas, including Kintail in Wester Ross in 1944. This property included the Five Sisters of Kintail, Ben Attow (Beinn Fhada), Glen Shiel and Loch Duich. In 1943 he set up the Mountainous Country Trust which enabled the NTS to buy Ben Lawers, with its outstanding Arctic mountain flora, Goatfell on Arran, and the untamed wilderness of the Torridon Estate.

It has been estimated that Unna's gifts and fundraising for NTS over his lifetime would be worth many millions of pounds today, and his Rules were praised by no less a conservationist than the Prince of Wales when he addressed the John Muir Trust AGM in 1991.

Having previously suffered a heart attack and after warnings about his future climbing activities, Unna died on 27 December 1950 of heart failure after a fall below the 3,245-foot Beinn Eunaich, between Loch Etive and Glen Strae. He had apparently arrived early for the SMC's New Year meeting at Dalmally but in truth died in a way he might have wished for. Ross Higgins, the SMC representative on the NTS Council, reported later: "Those who found his body said that his face carried the smile of a happy and contented man."

Unna is buried in a simple grave overlooking his beloved hills in the Pennyfuir Cemetery near Oban. His simple epitaph reads: "A great lover of the hills". In his obituary in the *Alpine Journal*, his former climbing partner Dr Finzi recalled: "We shall all miss Unna. No longer shall we hear that unique laugh. No longer shall we have those trenchant criticisms, so often right and so often pointing out defects that others had not observed."

The NTS president, the Earl of Wemyss and March, wrote of Unna in 1976:

> Behind the munificence of this remarkable man there was a simple motive. He appreciated, as few others did in the 1930s, that we have in the Highlands of Scotland, one of the last large reserves of wild and semi-wild land in Europe. He apprehended a threat which is now a stark reality – intolerable pressure on areas which are easy of access to a motorised population, and determined that so far as his resources and the wit of the Trust could provide for protection and temperate use, the high places would remain for the pleasure and refreshment of the man on foot.
>
> The 'Unna Rules' which he formulated some time before his death in 1950 have a certain spartan simplicity. I pray that we shall be able to abide by them.

One of his most ardent disciples was my good old friend, the late Rennie McOwan (see Chapter 11), who served as deputy press secretary with the NTS for many years. McOwan wrote of Unna:

> There is no man-made out-of-doors monument to him; no cairn or plaque on a prominent knoll or beside a road or path in Glencoe, Kintail or any of the other areas he knew so well. And that is how he would have wanted it. An outdoor monument, in his opinion, would have been desecration of the landscape.
>
> However, there is a living monument – the climbers and walkers – many of whom have never heard of him but who pay him an unconscious tribute and vote for him with their feet by climbing and walking, unhindered, in some of Scotland's finest mountain areas.

# The Unna Rules

1.  That "primitive" means not less primitive that the existing state.

2.  That sheep farming and cattle grazing may continue, but that deer stalking must cease, and no sport of any kind be carried on, or sporting rights sold or let; any use of the property for sport being wholly incompatible with the intention that the public should have unrestricted access and use. It is understood, however, that deer may have to be shot, as that may be necessary to keep down numbers and so prevent damage, but for that purpose alone.

3.  That the word "unrestricted" does not exclude regulations, but implies that regulations, if any, should be limited to such as may in future be found absolutely necessary, and be in sympathy with the views expressed herein.

4.  That the hills should not be made easier or safer to climb.

5.  That no facilities should be introduced for mechanical transport; that paths should not be extended or improved; and that new paths should not be made.

6. · That no directional or other signs, whether signposts, paint marks, cairns, or of any other kind whatever, should be allowed; with the exception of such signs as may be necessary to indicate that the land is the property of the Trust, and to give effect to the requirement in the Provisional Order of 1935 that by-laws must be exhibited.

7.  That should a demand spring up for hotels or hostels it is possible that it may have to be satisfied to a limited extent. If so, they should only be built alongside the public roads, and should be subject to control by the Trust; and it is suggested that no hotels or hostels should be built in Glencoe itself, or on any other part of the property, except, perhaps, in the lower reaches of the Trust property in Glen Etive. It is hoped that the Trust may be able to come to an understanding with the neighbouring proprietors as to corresponding restrictions being maintained in regard to land near to that held by the Trust.

8. That no other facilities should be afforded for obtaining lodging, shelter, food or drink; and, especially, that no shelters of any kind be built on the hills.

9. It is hoped that the design of any buildings which may be necessary will be carefully considered by the Trust; and that where possible, trees will be planted in their vicinity.

10. In conclusion, it is suggested that the whole question of the management of the Trust properties in Glen Etive and Glencoe should receive special attention, in view of the possibility that the policy adopted by the National Trust for Scotland in the present instance may create a precedent for similar areas in other mountainous districts, not only in Scotland, but also in England and Wales.

# 6: He Did It His Way
## Tom Stephenson (1893-1987)

**"AYE,"** SAID TOM STEPHENSON, A warm smile creasing his lined, weather-beaten face. "It's a grand valley isn't it?"

We were looking up Grindsbrook Clough to the rock rimmed Upper Tor and the heights of Kinder Scout, the highest ground in the Peak District. This was where it had all begun. The Pennine Way snakes northwards for 268 miles from here to Kirk Yetholm beyond the Scottish Border, keeping to the upper vertebrae of England's backbone all the way.

Stephenson, then a sprightly, even impish, eighty-three, was back in Edale as a speaker at a footpath preservation conference held

Tom Stephenson (left) with the author in Grindsbrook, Edale in 1976 (Peak District National Park)

at the now sadly lost National Park Study Centre at Losehill Hall, Castleton, in the summer of 1976. He had taken time off to see his much-loved Way after an absence of about twelve months. But when forty-one years before Stephenson had first proposed in a throwaway centre-spread filler for the *Daily Herald*, "a faint line… which the feet of grateful pilgrims would engrave on the face of the land," he could have had no idea of what would follow.

The story of how the paper received a letter from two American girls asking for advice about a walking holiday in England is now part of rambling mythology. They wondered if there was anything similar to their Appalachian Trail, which runs for 2,000 miles from Maine to Georgia, or the John Muir

Trail, running for 2,500 miles from the Canadian border through Washington, Oregon and California.

Stephenson's seminal article in response, headed "WANTED – A Long Green Trail", was published on 22 June 1935 and first proposed "a Pennine Way from the Peak to the Cheviots". He explained: "This need be no Euclidean line, but a meandering way deviating as needs be to include the best of that long range of moor and fell; no concrete or asphalt track, but just a faint line on the Ordnance Maps which the feet of grateful pilgrims would, with the passing years, engrave on the face of the land."

But didn't the four-lane "motorway" which the feet of those grateful pilgrims had worn in the eleven years since the final adoption of the Pennine Way offend him now, I wondered?

"Not at all," he responded in that warm Lancashire burr. "It's no more ugly than the peat groughs or scree slopes on Kinder, and it's just as natural as a sheep track worn by those animals. The whole idea was that the Pennine Way should not be a 'made' path; 'no concrete or asphalt track', as I said in the original article. No," he said looking down at the 'motorway', "This doesn't offend me – Constable would have loved it, it adds a bit of colour to the valley." He was less complimentary, however, about the black plastic matting which had recently been laid to combat erosion on the route north of the Snake Summit.

"The way I see it is that this route has given so much pleasure to so many thousands of people who perhaps otherwise would not have ventured onto the hills," said Stephenson. "This is what I wanted in the first place, and when I see young people enjoying themselves on the Way, it makes it all seem worthwhile."

There had been a mounting wave of criticism in mountaineering circles against the designation of all forms of long-distance footpaths. A proposed Cambrian Way and a long-distance route in the Cairngorms had attracted a storm of protest. Were there not too many "ways" now? "Mountaineers were always opposed to the Pennine Way," he recalled. "*The Times* complained that ramblers were being mollycoddled when the Pennine Way was first proposed. But if having a designated 'way' has meant more people enjoying the freedom of the hills,

I can't see anything wrong in that." But he added: "Perhaps the time has come when we have got enough."

Talking to Stephenson about the inception of the Pennine Way, and the setting up of the National Parks Commission, you realise how important fate plays in these things. He had been the right man in the right place at the right time. It is doubtful whether any of this important legislation by the post-war Labour government would have passed onto the Statute Book had not all these conditions have been in place at the time.

Stephenson's face lit up and his tongue darted out mischievously as he recounted the tales of a judiciously-worded press release written with *carte blanche* ministerial consent, and the publicity-seeking walks with leading Cabinet ministers along sections of his proposed Pennine Way – all arranged when he was Press Officer to the Ministry of Town and Country Planning just after the war. "Aye, we had some fun," he grinned.

In an echo of John Muir's (see Chapter 3) introduction of President Roosevelt to the wonders of Yosemite in 1903, one of Stephenson's boldest and most effective stunts was the three-day walk in 1948 along the proposed route of his Pennine Way for a group of Cabinet members and prominent north-eastern MPs in Clement Atlee's Labour government. The walk took in the splendours of Teesdale, High Cup Nick, Cross Fell and Hadrian's Wall.

The party included Barbara Castle, MP for Blackburn (later Baroness Castle), who became the first female Secretary of State and

Tom Stephenson leads MPs on his proposed Pennine Way

later Minister of Transport in Harold Wilson's government; Fred Willey, MP for Sunderland; Arthur Blenkinsop, MP for Newcastle East and South Shields; George Chetwynd, MP for Stockton; and Hugh Dalton, MP for Bishop Auckland and until recently Chancellor of the Exchequer. Also in the group was Julian Snow, who later became Baron Burntwood.

All of the group were walkers themselves and many held positions in the Ramblers' Association as well as senior positions in various national wildlife and conservation bodies. It was largely their efforts which led in 1949 to the National Parks and Access to the Countryside Act. It is difficult to imagine such a group of senior MPs of any political persuasion now taking part in such a stunt involving such strenuous outdoor activity.

Stephenson recalled that at the time the Ministry was "a cheerless place" permeated with a fear of publicity. "John Dower (see Chapter 8) was my only kindred spirit and publicising his famous National Parks Report in 1945 was one of the most satisfying tasks I ever had," he confessed in *Forbidden Land* (1989).

He frankly admitted that one of the major reasons behind the route of the Pennine Way in its southern section was to clear up the longstanding problems of access over Kinder Scout and Bleaklow. When the route was first proposed, only 180 miles were on existing rights of way, leaving about seventy miles of new rights of way to be negotiated. Half of these were in the Kinder-Bleaklow section. Stephenson had some horrifying tales to tell of the old access battles fought between ramblers and gamekeepers on the moors of the Dark Peak, and he kept a weighty dossier of gamekeeper assaults during that period.

An inveterate trespasser himself, Stephenson was always vehemently opposed to the Mass Trespass of 1932, and he never saw eye-to-eye with Benny Rothman, its Young Communist leader (see Chapter 10). One of my greatest achievements when I was Head of Information Services at the Peak District National Park was to get Stephenson and Rothman to speak from the same platform at a National Park rally which I organised in Cavedale, Castleton in 1986.

Stephenson often told me he thought the best thing to come from the Mass Trespass was Ewan MacColl's celebrated ramblers' anthem, "The Manchester Rambler", which he said perfectly encapsulated the trespassing spirit, and which is still sung every year at the conclusion of the Spirit of Kinder celebrations.

*

It was seventy years before our first meeting that Stephenson had experienced his introduction to the hills. One crisp March morning when he was just thirteen, equipped only with his wooden clogs, he stood for the first time on a mountain summit. He climbed to the witch-haunted 1,830-foot summit of Pendle Hill from his home in the mill town of Whalley in the Ribble Valley of Lancashire The memory of that crystal-clear morning was still as fresh to Stephenson then as if it had been yesterday. To the south he said he could see the serried ranks of factories, their chimneys belching out smoke which blanketed towns like Nelson, Colne and Burnley. But looking north, he said: "It was just wild country, nothing at all. And the great attraction was that so easily you lost any sense of industrialisation or civilisation; you felt you were alone in the world. It was simply breathtaking," he recalled. "I saw range after range of snow-capped hills – Ingleborough, Penyghent, Whernside – all of which I didn't know then, but which were to become old friends."

"Oh gosh," he added, that impish smile again flashing across his face, "I just hadn't realised that this whole new world was on my doorstep and I made up my mind that day that this was for me."

Stephenson came from a working-class family, the eldest of nine children, and started work at the age of thirteen as an apprentice block printer in the same calico printing works as his father. The nine-bob (45p) a 66-hour week apprentice printer walked the Pennines from Dovedale to Hadrian's Wall in his days off during the next few years and got to know them intimately. Although he wrote the first official guide, he admitted he had personally never walked the whole length of his Pennine Way in one continuous trip, as neither did Alfred Wainwright, the author of its most popular guide.

He started writing about his walks and in his spare time studied geology at evening classes at Burnley Technical School, with the ambition of winning a scholarship to the Royal College of Science in London. His hard work and determination paid off in 1915 when he won one of only two scholarships awarded nationally for geology by the Board of Education.

However, the First World War intervened and Stephenson, who had opposed the war in principle from its very outbreak, became a conscientious objector. He was arrested, forced to join the East Lancashire Regiment but court martialled and sentenced to twelve months' hard labour at Wormwood Scrubs. Later, after a second court martial, he served two years in Northallerton Prison, and his scholarship award was rescinded.

Stephenson used his time in prison well, reading everything from Edward Gibbons *Decline and Fall of the Roman Empire* to John Stuart Mill's *System of Logic*. He told me in later years he was at a posh function when "a toff" asked him if he ever been to Northallerton? "Yes," he replied to the sound of dropping jaws, "I was in prison there."

Justice was finally done, however, when Stephenson was awarded an honorary degree by the University of Lancaster for his services to literature and access to the countryside in 1986. One of my most treasured possessions is a photograph which Stephenson sent me of him standing proudly in his degree gown and mortar board in his living room.

He met his wife of over fifty years, Madge, shortly after the war. She became what is known in the conservation business as an "amenity widow". Once when she came round in hospital after a minor operation, she found a neighbour waiting to take her home rather than Stephenson. "Where's Tom?" enquired the neighbour. "He'd be here if I was a National Park," she answered ruefully. Madge died in 1982.

In October 1919, Stephenson returned to his trade of block printing in London, and became closely involved in the Independent Labour Party, eventually becoming a part-time agent for the ILP. In 1933, on the invitation of Ernest Bevin, he became a journalist for the *Daily Herald* and editor of a TUC-controlled magazine called *Hiker and Camper* and writing about his first love of walking in the countryside.

At the same time, he first became involved with the National Council of Ramblers' Federations, covering its annual conference at Ilkley in 1933. The following year he was invited to speak at the annual Access to Mountains rally held in The Winnats Pass outside Castleton in the Peak District. He recalled: "As a writer, I panicked at the thought of addressing 3,000 ramblers seemingly glued to a perpendicular hillside. But I was inspired by the enthusiasm and dedication of the young folk who were campaigning for the right to walk on their native hills, the preservation of footpaths and the creation of National Parks."

After working as press officer at the Ministry of Town and Country Planning and for the Hobhouse Committee, which in 1947 produced the recommendations for National Parks following the Dower Report, Stephenson became the first full-time secretary of the Ramblers' Association from 1948 for over twenty years, also serving on the National Parks Commission and the Gosling Committee into the development of a better system of paths and bridle ways

When the honorary secretary of the Ramblers' Association resigned, Stephenson offered to fill the post temporarily, never imagining that it would be his job for the next two decades. "Crowded years they have been," he recalled in *Forbidden Land*, "Writing, lecturing, arguing, going on deputations to Ministers, giving evidence at public enquiries and spending innumerable hours on a multitude of committees."

His final gift to the Ramblers was that when he died at the age of ninety-four in 1987, he left most of what he owned to the walking charity, including a generous legacy – the largest ever received by the association at the time. During our walk on the Pennine Way more than four decades ago, it was obvious that the attraction of the hills was still as strong. He was looking forward to a walking holiday in the Lakes when we met, keenly anticipating a reunion with his favourite hill, Glaramara – "not too high, but nice and knobbly".

A television documentary once renamed the Pennine Way "Stephenson's Way", and although Stephenson would never have accepted that self-aggrandising title, it seemed a fitting tribute to his imaginative concept of Britain's first National Trail.

**Based on the author's interview with Tom Stephenson in** *Peak Park News*, **journal of the Peak District National Park, Autumn 1976.**

Stephenson (centre) with Benny Rothman (left) and Stephen Morton at the Cavedale Rally, 1986 (Peak District National Park)

# 7: Guardians of the Peak
## Gerald (1912-95) & Ethel (1894-1986) Haythornthwaite

WHEN I FIRST JOINED THE staff of the Peak District National Park Joint Planning Board in 1975, fellow officers spoke in awe of "the Big Three" among the governing membership.

They were the long-standing, straight-talking Chairman of the Board, Alderman Norman Gratton from Tideswell, who represented Derbyshire County Council; Ivor Morten, a conservationist and farmer from Burbage, near Buxton, the jovial, urbane chairman of the Park Management Committee; and "Colonel H" – as Lt. Col. Gerald Haythornthwaite was known – the hard-line Chairman of the all-important Planning Control Committee. These three men were largely responsible for formulating the pioneering policies of Britain's first National Park in its earliest years.

And if Haythornthwaite had been looking for a motto, he could have done worse than choose the quotation used in the 1956 Annual Report of the Sheffield and Peak District branch of the Council (now Campaign) for the Protection of Rural England (CPRE). Referring to the successful blocking of a 200 mph Grand Prix motor racing circuit around Hartington, it quoted the Earl of Cambridge in William Shakespeare's *Henry V*, Act II, Scene 2: "But God be thanked for prevention."

Conservationists would do well to extend their thanks to the Almighty to include the former Territorial Army Lieutenant Colonel who did as much as anyone to protect the Peak District National Park from harmful development through its early years. His reputation as an uncompromising conservationist was reflected in a successful battle to stop a sports pavilion being built near the Eagle Stone on Baslow Edge. "God," said John Foster, then the Chief Planning Officer, "you would stop anything!"

## WALKING CLASS HEROES

It was fitting that "Colonel H's" quarter century of service to the National Park should end on what was arguably the greatest victory in his campaigning career. The cancellation of the still regularly proposed motorway-standard trans-Pennine route through Longdendale in 1977 was, in his own words, "probably the most important decision in the history of the National Park".

He described to me in an interview published in *Peak Park News* in 1977 the twelve-year battle which he had waged as Chairman of the National Park's Planning Committee, and also as technical advisor to the Sheffield and Peak branch of CPRE, to stop the new road. "If it had gone through," he warned, "it would have created the most dangerous precedent – the first motorway-type route through any National Park."

Although it apparently was the economic arguments which swayed the Secretary of State's ultimate decision, Haythornthwaite was sure that the pressure exerted by amenity groups must have also influenced him. His inspired photographic superimposition of the proposed sweeping motorway viaduct over the River Etherow in the wild Longdendale valley graphically illustrated the point, and undoubtedly played a large part in the decision.

The other milestones of Haythornthwaite's success as the unflinching "Guardian of the Peak" included opposition to that Hartington Grand Prix circuit, which would have required parking for 25,000 cars and twenty-foot high crash barriers through the sensitive White Peak scenery around the Neolithic stone circle of Arbor Low; blocking a proposed reservoir at Hassop, opposed by people as influential as the Poet Laureate John Betjeman; and supporting the re-use of the old Woodhead railway tunnel, again in Longdendale, for undergrounding the 40Kv power line which otherwise would have marched on huge pylons across the unsullied moorland.

*

Gerald Haythornthwaite was born in the Lancashire mill town of Bolton and went to the independent Bolton School. It was school scoutmaster Bill Brooks who introduced the young Haythornthwaite to the countryside, through regular camping trips to the West Pennine Moors, the Lake District and Wales. Brooks also took his boys abroad, with trips to Normandy, Spain and the Pyrenees, including a rather scary trip up to the impressive Brèche de Roland pass above Gavarnie in the Ordesa y Monte Perdido National Park.

After leaving school, Haythornthwaite studied for his chosen profession of architecture on a five-year-course at Manchester University, eventually winning a position with Sir Percy Worthington's practice in central Manchester.

Haythornthwaite's introduction to the Peak came through rock climbing on the gritstone edges like Stanage after he had moved to Sheffield in 1935, first to work for the City Architect and later in private practice. He was a member of the Sheffield Pennine Club and the Rucksack Club in the 1920s and 1930s and he told me he was involved in many deliberate trespasses on Kinder Scout and Bleaklow in those days.

Gerald Haythornthwaite on Chrome Hill in the Upper Dove valley
(Friends of the Peak/CPRE)

It was then he became involved in CPRE. His wife-to-be, Ethel Gallimore, was the founding secretary of the Peak branch at the time and had served on the Hobhouse Committee on National Parks. After being interviewed by his future wife, Haythornthwaite became the branch's assistant secretary on a salary of £250 per annum in 1936.

After eighteen months during which they had become romantically involved, he diplomatically resigned his position and took up a post in Sheffield City Council's Architects' Department. The couple married in December 1937 and they spent their honeymoon in Swaledale in the northern Yorkshire Dales. Gerald returned to CPRE Sheffield as technical secretary two years later, shortly before being called up with his Territorial Army unit at the outbreak of the Second World War.

In addition to proposing and vigorously protecting the Sheffield Green Belt, both Haythornthwaites were involved in the National Park movement from the very start. Through CPRE, they drew up the first map showing a suggested park boundary as early as 1938. Gerald and Ethel were often to be found out exploring the boundaries of the prospective new National Park. The proposed legislation for the new park was drawn up by the Joint Standing Committee on National Parks, in consultation with other amenity groups such as CPRE, long before the designation of the park in 1951.

Ethel Haythornthwaite speaking at an access rally in The Winnats, Castleton (Friends of the Peak/CPRE)

Ethel, the daughter of Sheffield steel magnate Thomas Ward, was a founding member in 1924 of the Sheffield Association for the Preservation of Local Scenery, later to become the Sheffield and South Yorkshire branch of the Council (now Campaign) to Protect Rural England (now the Friends of the Peak). She was always a lover and keen lone explorer, often on her horse Bracken, of the beauties of the Peak District, which forms the western boundary of the Steel City's "Golden Frame". In her 1926 poem, "The Pride of the Peak", she expressed this deeply held affection in a description of a trespass on Froggatt Edge:

> *I will go up, I will go all alone*
> *Up to the moors, the blue and cloudy sky;*
> *Even to those fierce rands of blackened stone*
> *Whose ramparts sharp across the moorland lie:*
> *Where lies the water black and cold,*
> *Where gleams the bracken tipped with gold,*
> *Beside the grasses pale and by the sedge,*
> *On high above the cliffs of Froggatt Edge.*

Gerald Haythornthwaite became a Secretary of State nominee to the inaugural Peak Park Joint Planning Board in 1951 through his association with CPRE. He recalled to me with a smile those first meetings, when nominated and elected members sat on either side of the table – "revolvers at the ready". There were a few stormy clashes in those days, as the authority was feeling its way towards its groundbreaking new policies.

Being the first in the field created its own problems, of course. "In my view, the Peak was the crucible for all the other National Parks," Haythornthwaite told me. "All the access problems were concentrated in the Peak, and others have since followed the example of our access agreements. The same applies to traffic schemes like the Goyt Valley... The battle for the Peak District National Park had been going on since the 1920s, and the pressure on it from various quarters had been growing during all this time. I do believe that the successes we have had in this National Park will provide a pattern for the others."

What about his reputation as "the king of the Peak District conservationists" I asked? "We want the highest standards as we are setting the standards for others, so I don't think we can afford to compromise," he said. "The standard of development throughout the country since the war has been pretty low, and I believe it shows a national malaise among architects.

"But I do think local people should be consulted over developments," he added. "You will always get friction at local level, and I don't think you can get out of it."

When he was awarded an honorary MA from the University of Sheffield in 1963, the public orator described Haythornthwaite as "the custodian of our natural beauty and arbiter of architectural elegance." He was awarded a CBE for his outstanding services to the Peak Park Joint Planning Board in the 1970 New Year's Honours List. Ethel had already been made an MBE for her services to countryside conservation in 1947, and when she was awarded an honorary MA from the University of Sheffield in 1951, the orator described her as "a sleepless guardian of the beauty of the countryside". She carried on as secretary of the Sheffield branch of CPRE until 1980 and she died aged ninety-two in April 1986 after a long period of ill health.

After Gerald Haythornthwaite left the National Park Board in 1977, he continued in his watchdog role through CPRE, the Voluntary Joint Committee for the Peak District National Park and the Standing Committee on National Parks, of which he was chairman for several years.

His abiding love of the outdoors and his commitment to freedom to roam were perhaps best expressed in an interview he did with Marion Shoard (see Chapter 16) in her chapter on "The Lure of the Moors" in *Valued Environments* (Allen and Unwin, 1982):

Man has need of direct personal relationship with his natural surroundings in which he can enjoy the grandeur and the richness of land and sea and feel the force of the elements.

A man is only half a man who cannot exult in a storm on a moor, or a mountain top, or in the sea, or be enraptured at the sight of a squirrel on the garden wall, or a fox in the field. Without such things I believe we shall lose contact with the source of all fresh inspiration. As something "natural" and as the antithesis of the man-made world, wilderness provides a perspective on city life and the human condition more generally.

To find our true unaverage status, the unique importance that each individual possesses but which the world denies, we must have places where we can withdraw and be remote from men and their material works and be enfolded by the natural order of things, able to feel that one can go back to the start and unravel the false conclusions of this and other ages.

Gerald Haythornthwaite died at the age of eighty-two after coming in to work as usual in his office at The Stables in Endcliffe Crescent, Sheffield on 4 January 1995 – coincidentally almost fifty-nine years to the day when he had first started work in Sheffield. The national chairman of CPRE, Lord Marlesford, described him as "a unique and dedicated champion of the countryside, whose reputation and influence are unparalleled by anyone today". Speaking at his memorial service, Fiona Reynolds (see Chapter 19), then national director of CPRE, spoke of his "enormous zeal for the task" and his "tirelessness and dauntless approach in the face of seemingly insurmountable obstacles".

Ethel and Gerald Haythornthwaite (Friends of the Peak/CPRE)

## WALKING CLASS HEROES

As Britain's first National Park in the Peak District prepares to celebrate its seventieth anniversary in 2021, it owes an enormous debt of gratitude to the pioneering work of "Colonel H" and his wife Ethel, the original and pioneering Guardians of the Peak.

**Based on the author's interview with Gerald Haythornthwaite in** *Peak Park News*, **journal of the Peak District National Park, Summer 1977.**

# 8: Architect of the National Parks
## John Dower (1900-47)

**THE GREAT IRONY OF THE** tragically short life of John Dower, the man who wrote the blueprint for the British system of National Parks, was that he never lived to see its implementation in the 1949 National Parks and Access to the Countryside Act.

A long-time sufferer from tuberculosis, he died at the early age of forty-seven at Cambo House, close to his wife's family home of Wallington in Northumberland, on 3 October 1947, just seventeen months before the Minister of Town and Country Planning, Lewis Silkin, opened the second reading of the Act in the Houses of Parliament on 31 March 1949.

Silkin told the Commons: "In 1945 the late Mr John Dower issued a report on National Parks in England and Wales. He was a great champion of the open air, and it is a source of deep regret to us all that he has not survived to see the fruition of his efforts; but his work lives on."

Silkin was later to become famous for his "Silkin Test," under which if there was a conflict between conservation and development and there was no practicable alternative, conservation should always come first.

Silkin made clear his pride in presenting the 1949 Act, which he called:

> … a people's charter for the open air, for the hikers and the ramblers, for everyone who loves to get out into the open air and enjoy the countryside. Without if they are fettered, deprived of their powers of access and facilities needed to make holidays enjoyable. With it the countryside is theirs to preserve, to cherish, to enjoy and to make their own.

Silkin also acknowledged the long history of pressure for access to open country, particularly to the grouse moors of the Peak District, scene of the access battles of the 1930s. "I propose accordingly to enable planning authorities to declare a public right of access to specified areas of uncultivated land, including beach and foreshore, where there is reason to think that the public are unreasonably excluded; and I would propose to provide for compensation…"

This put the long-cherished right to roam for walkers and ramblers in open country into the hands of local planning authorities and not the National Park authorities through the newly-proposed National Parks Commission (later to become the Countryside Commission and later still the Countryside Agency), as Dower had proposed. In practice, three-quarters of all the access agreements in Britain were made by the Peak District National Park Authority – guardians of the scene of the trespasses of the 1930s – which exercised the right through the negotiation of access agreements with moorland owners. The only other major exception was on the Duke of Devonshire's Bolton Abbey estate in the Yorkshire Dales National Park.

Although the Act gave us our current system of National Parks and National Trails, the passing of the 1947 Town and Country Planning Act had seriously weakened Dower's visionary blueprint, in most cases giving planning powers to constituent local planning authorities rather than to the Park authorities themselves.

However, a total of ten National Parks were established between 1951 and 1957 from Dower's so-called "A" list. They were: The Peak District, the Lake District, Snowdonia and Dartmoor (1951); the Pembrokeshire Coast and the North York Moors (1952); the Yorkshire Dales and Exmoor (1954); Northumberland (1956) and the Brecon Beacons (1957). Since then, the Norfolk & Suffolk Broads (1989); Loch Lomond & the Trossachs (2002); the Cairngorms (2003); the New Forest (2005); and most recently, in 2010, the South Downs have joined the family.

# 8: ARCHITECT OF THE NATIONAL PARKS

In his beautifully written 1945 report, Dower came up with the classic definition of a British National Park:

A National Park may be defined, in application to Great Britain, as an extensive area of beautiful and relatively wild country in which, for the nation's benefit and by appropriate national decision and action:
a) the characteristic landscape beauty is strictly preserved
b) access and facilities for public open-air enjoyment are amply provided
c) wildlife and buildings and places of architectural and historic interest are suitably protected, while
d) established farming use is effectively maintained.

These aims were amended and condensed by the Environment Act of 1995 as follows:

- to conserve and enhance the natural beauty, wildlife and cultural heritage of the National Parks and
- to promote opportunities for the understanding and enjoyment of the special qualities of the National Parks by the public.

The National Park authorities also now have an additional duty to foster the economic and social wellbeing of their local communities in pursuit of these purposes.

*

John Dower was born into a comfortable upper middle-class Victorian family in the shadow of the Cow and Calf Rocks on the edge of Ilkley Moor, in Wharfedale, West Yorkshire, the first child of Robert Dower and his wife Mary. Robert Dower was the chairman of a Leeds steel merchant, a keen rambler and a Methodist lay preacher.

With his father and younger brother Arthur, John was introduced to his love of the countryside by exploring Ilkley

Moor, with its famous examples of prehistoric rock art, and the moors and dales around Wharfedale, and later on walking holidays both at home and abroad. Arthur was later to become chairman of the Youth Hostels Association and a member of the Yorkshire Dales National Park Authority.

John Dower was educated at a local preparatory school in Ilkley and at the age of thirteen followed in his father's footsteps to The Leys School and then on to St John's College, Cambridge. The outbreak of the First World War in 1914 saw Dower joining The Leys' Officer Training Corps and it was only the Armistice in 1918 which spared him from being sent to the Western Front in France.

The same year he passed the entrance exam and was offered a Foundation Scholarship to St John's in Cambridge. In what would now be called a "gap year", Dower spent three months in northern France, which was still recovering from the ravages of four years of war. There he lodged with a French priest with what his family believed would ultimately lead to fatal consequences. The *curé* was apparently suffering from some kind of respiratory disease, which could well have been the tuberculosis bacteria which was rampant in France at the time, and which eventually was to be the cause of Dower's premature death.

Dower was a star pupil at Cambridge, gaining two firsts in the Historical Tripos in 1921, and in a BA in Architectural Construction and Architecture. In his final examinations in 1923 he gained an Upper Second Class in History and a Second in History of Art for his Ordinary degree.

He had joined the Department of Architecture at Cambridge in 1922 under George Pepler, his lifelong mentor and friend, who was to become godfather to Dower's eldest son Michael. Here he also came under the influence of Patrick Abercrombie, the distinguished town planner and Britain's first Professor of Architecture at Liverpool University.

In order to qualify as a Royal Institute of British Architects (RIBA) Associate, Dower spent the next five years with the Herbert Bell practice in Westminster, where he was involved with several major projects including serving on the RIBA's

Aerodromes Committee, which looked into the planning implications of what were then known as "landing fields". It was at about this time that Dower became part of one of the most famous expressions of the Liberal Trevelyan family's legendary love of the countryside. This was annual "Man Hunt" in the hills of what was later to become what many claim to be England's most beautiful National Park, the Lake District.

As David Cannadine relates in his 1992 biography of the great historian GM Trevelyan, "Every Whitsuntide, the finest flower of the new Liberal intelligentsia descended on the Lake District, usually at Seatoller, sometimes at Stool End, near Langdale." Loosely modelled on the Harrow public school game of hare and hounds (with which many of the participants would have been familiar), the Man Hunt was founded in 1898 by Trevelyan, top rock climber Geoffrey Winthrop Young and engineer Sidney McDougall, who was killed at Gallipoli in 1915. It was apparently inspired by the account of the pursuit of Alan Stewart in Robert Louis Stevenson's popular 1886 novel *Kidnapped*. The group was divided into two groups, and after the nominated "hares" had set off, the "hounds" followed, literally hunting them down over three days and nights over about ten square miles of the fells.

Other Liberal-leaning dignitaries who were invited included Cabinet minister and access campaigner Sir Charles Trevelyan; Chancellor of the Exchequer Hugh Dalton; Home Secretary Herbert Samuel; William Beveridge, later to write his famous report on the National Health Service; and philosopher Professor Cyril Joad of BBC Radio's popular Brains Trust.

Twenty-five-year-old John Dower, maternal nephew to Trevelyan and later to become son-in-law to Sir Charles Trevelyan, was invited to join the Trevelyan Man Hunt at Seatoller in Borrowdale in 1925. According to his biographer, David Wilkinson, with his six foot four lanky frame and long legs, Dower proved to be ideally suited to running, leaping and scrambling over the steep fellsides. He managed to catch a hare on his first outing, adding an average of one a year during his fourteen years with the Man Hunt.

The meeting with Charles Trevelyan was also to prove fateful for Dower, as the day after his twenty-ninth birthday he was married to the former's oldest daughter Pauline, an accomplished artist and a keen conservationist herself, who later served on the National Park Commission which designated the new National Parks.

Charles Trevelyan was a member of Ramsay MacDonald's first Labour Cabinet. In 1908, he had been one of the prime movers behind an unsuccessful Access to Mountains and Moorland Bill, one of the earliest attempts to open the uplands to walkers, and a forerunner of the Countryside and Rights of Way Act 2000 which finally allowed the right of roam in England.

Dower's second son, Michael, former director of the Countryside Commission and my old boss as chief executive of the Peak District National Park Authority, related how his father had bought into "the family business" by marrying into the Trevelyans.

> They were all involved in the business of seeking to protect wild areas. That was their passion. So they got hold of this young man who had just married Charles Trevelyan's daughter and said to him, "You must come and help us with our work."
>
> From that moment on, my father became the drafting secretary of the Council (now Campaign) for Rural England's crusade for the establishment of National Parks, working alongside people like Patrick Abercrombie, one of CPRE's founders, and Pennine Way creator Tom Stephenson.

John and Pauline Dower bought a house in Ilkley, but he continued to have to make frequent visits to London to continue his work. Dower had published his first pamphlet *The Case for National Parks*, arguing the case, while the first unsatisfactory Creech Jones Access to the Mountains Act was passed in 1938. This legislation still contained many restrictions including a hated trespass clause, making it a criminal offence to be on open moorland. Yet just before the outbreak of the Second World War, the principle of National Parks was becoming more generally accepted.

Pen and ink drawing of John Dower by Pauline Dower

Inevitably, when war came in 1939, everything was put on hold. John volunteered for the Royal Engineers and, putting his skills as an architect to use, was given the job of strengthening the coastal defences at Dover. But when the winter arrived, he became ill and was first diagnosed with tuberculosis. By early 1940 he was so ill that he had to be invalided out of service.

By this stage he and Pauline had three children; Susan, Michael and Robin, who became a well-known architect, a member of the Northumberland National Park Committee and of the Countryside Commission in the 1980s. When the Luftwaffe bombing raids on London began, as much as for their safety as for his health the family took a lease on a house called The Rookery in the Yorkshire Dales village of Kirkby Malham.

On some days Dower was well enough to make the short journey up to the impressive limestone amphitheatre of Malham Cove, but he spent a lot of time convalescing in bed at The Rookery. As he gazed out of his upstairs window and across the fields of Malhamdale he occasionally wrote articles for *The Dalesman* magazine. In one piece, Dower vented his frustration at the lack of progress on his pre-war report arguing the need for National Parks. "There's no point in making plans merely to fill dusty pigeonholes," he wrote. "In open-air recreation and the preservation of our 'green and pleasant land', how much effort there has been for how little assured achievement!"

In 1942, however, he learned that his National Parks report had been accepted by the government. Unable to play any part in the war, Dower was given the task of turning his concept into firm proposals. But the tuberculosis had left him too weak to drive, which made it difficult if not impossible for him to visit all the landscapes he needed to survey.

So his wife, Pauline, became his unpaid chauffeur. In the family's blue and silver Vauxhall 10 – and with special dispensation petrol rations provided by Whitehall – she drove him from Northumberland to Dartmoor, and all round England and Wales to visit his prospective National Parks.

Michael Dower, who regrettably hardly knew his father while he was away at preparatory school, recalled: "My father knew the proposed National Parks pretty well. I can still remember them going off in our old Vauxhall with its fluted bonnet. He was reappraising the landscape according to the

Ilkley Moor (David Wilkinson)

definition he had worked out for the parks, which was basically areas of beautiful and relatively wild country. That was the crucial central phrase."

Dower's report was completed in 1943 but not published until after the war. Sadly, by 1947 when a government committee chaired by Sir Arthur Hobhouse was set up to implement it, Dower had lost his long running battle against tuberculosis, and he died at The Rookery on 3 October 1947. In accordance with his wishes, his ashes were appropriately scattered near the prehistoric rock carving of the so-called Swastika Stone on Ilkley Moor, scene of some of the happiest moments of his childhood.

# 9: Shield of Dartmoor
## Lady Sylvia Sayer (1904-2000)

*There's an eloquent Dame*
*(I won't mention her name)*
*Who toils for the Moor's preservation.*
*Explosions from mortars*
*And reservoired waters*
*Call forth her most dire indignation.*
From Sir Henry Slesser, "Defensor forestae", in *This Barren Waste* (1966)

**IT IS A WELL-WORN GUIDEBOOK** cliché, but Dartmoor is often still called the last wilderness in southern Britain. When you stand on the wrinkled granite and boulder-strewn summits of Rough Tor or Great Mis Tor and look around at the rolling, tor-topped moorland, you can believe it, because Dartmoor is still largely wild and free.

And for this state of affairs, according to her protégée and successor, Kate Ashbrook, general secretary of the Open Spaces Society (see Chapter 18), we all owe a deep debt of gratitude to Sylvia Sayer, who devoted over half a century of her long life to defending Dartmoor's precious wilderness.

As the redoubtable chair of the Dartmoor Preservation Association for over twenty years, she defended the celebrated moorland with an uncompromising zeal, causing her opponents to quake in their boots whenever she appeared against them. Short of stature and latterly with a piratical black eye patch, Sayer earned both fear and respect in equal measure from everyone who dared to oppose her, whether they were bumbling bureaucrats, procrastinating politicians or devious developers.

Sayer was born in Plymouth in 1904 into a buttoned-up, upper middle-class Edwardian family. She scarcely knew her father, a naval surgeon, since he was so often at sea. Yet she had granite in her blood, not least because her mother came from farming stock on Cornwall's Bodmin Moor. And it was her maternal grandfather, Robert Burnard, founder of the Dartmoor Preservation Association in 1883, who was to have the greatest influence on the young Sayer. Among the major joys of her childhood were the regular visits she paid with her sister Phyllis to his home at Huccaby House, close to the centre of the moor near Princetown, which her grandfather leased from the landowner, the Duchy of Cornwall.

As Sayer wrote in 1973:

> It was a place of strong and potent magic: no children were ever happier than we were there. To be told we were "going to Huccaby" was to be seized with a kind of mad joy; to leave it was a cruel banishment.
>
> For me the Huccaby magic is still there, and I can forget today's packed cars and milling people around Huccaby Bridge, the car park in Huccaby Meadow and the litter floating in the Dart, and I'm back as a small grandchild staying at Huccaby House, with the lovely rushing voice of the river and the scent of the rhododendrons and pines blowing in at my bedroom window. And tomorrow would be bringing another wonderful Dartmoor day.

The River Dart at Hexworthy

Sayer married her naval officer husband Guy in 1925, and the newly married couple discovered Old Middle Cator, a tumble-down, heather-thatched cottage near Widecombe, in 1928. They bought Cator for the princely sum of £150 and happily lived there for the rest of their lives. In 1930, their twin sons, Oliver (Oz) and Geoff, were born, and grew up in that idyllic setting.

Shortly after Sayer married Guy he found himself stationed to Hong Kong, but she could not bear to be parted from him and so in 1949 she travelled to China. She persuaded *The Shanghai Times* that she was a war artist and the newspaper let her follow him up the River Yangtze, where the battle which became known as the Amethyst Incident was raging. Guy died in 1985.

It was after the war that Sayer found herself more deeply involved in the protection of Dartmoor. In 1951 she became chairman of the Dartmoor Preservation Association, founded by her grandfather, and built it up from 140 members to the effective pressure group that it is today. In 1973 she retired from the chair and she and Guy became patrons of the association.

There can be no doubt that Sayer played an important role in the establishment of the Dartmoor National Park, the fourth in Britain, in 1951, and she became a member of the park committee from 1952 until 1957. She resigned in protest at what she saw as the committee's failure to uphold essential national values. At the time, the park authority was a sub-committee of Devon County Council and controlled by a small cabal of aldermen.

The final straw for Sayer came when the chairman, Alderman Sir Henry Slesser, a former Solicitor-General (quoted at the head of this chapter) used his casting vote in favour of the expansion of china-clay mining in the park. At that time Dartmoor was facing a barrage of threats, not just from the expansion of china clay workings but also from the extension of military training on the Okehampton ranges, a huge 643-foot TV and radio mast on the 1,696-foot North Hessary Tor and the piecemeal ploughing and enclosure of what was formerly open country.

Sayer also served on the Standing Committee on National

Parks, now the Campaign for National Parks. She was a member of the Commons Preservation Society (now the Open Spaces Society) committee, giving up her post in 1978 to the current boss Kate Ashbrook. She also worked closely with the Ramblers' Association, where she was a vice-president, to win a better deal for greater public access for walkers on Dartmoor. She represented several of these bodies at Dartmoor's many public inquiries, some of which lasted for several months.

"Sayer was fearless in her cross-examination of those who proposed to damage the moor at these public inquiries," said Ashbrook. "She was never caught out when she herself was questioned, because her preparation of the case was impeccable and her knowledge of the moor unparalleled." Ashbrook summed up what she thought about her friend: "She did not care what people thought about her, so long as she did the right thing for Dartmoor. She battled calmly, courteously and effectively, with steadfast support from Guy... There were many who must have dreaded the beautifully-written envelope from her dropping through their letterbox. She never learned to type, and her copper-plate handwriting became her hallmark. Above all, Syl was tremendously courageous and resourceful."

An example of this courage occurred in 1967 when she walked across Ringmoor Down in south-west Dartmoor as military helicopters buzzed around her, to expose the danger to walkers and riders of their gun-dropping activities. She even painted a watercolour of the event, with a helicopter shown scattering a group of Dartmoor ponies. And she would often march across the northern Dartmoor military ranges during live firing to exercise what she said was "her common rights" of grazing and cutting peat there.

Sayer was also prepared to take on the establishment in the days when it was unfashionable to do so. In 1983, when Prince Charles as Duke of Cornwall invited her to Kensington Palace to celebrate the launch of the Duchy's management plan for Dartmoor, she turned down the invitation because the Prince had given no indication that he would be telling the military to stop using Dartmoor for live firing.

A particular arch-enemy of Sayer was the late Sir Peter Mills, Conservative MP for West Devon, who played an ignominious role in the destruction of the West Okement valley by the construction of the Meldon Reservoir. When Mills received his knighthood in 1982, Sayer, displaying her typically iconoclastic humour, immediately knighted her pet donkey "Sir Erastus".

Another opponent was Alderman Wilkey, whom she described as "a little Water Board Napoleon" in *The Meldon Story*, her account of the battle, on the day that work on the reservoir began in March 1970. Wilkey was photographed looking totally incongruous in the Dartmoor scene in his black Homburg hat and overcoat, as he posed for the photographers to celebrate his moment of triumph by pressing a button to blow up a tree. She also produced a scathing description of the band of bureaucrats who visited the site of the proposed Swincombe Reservoir in the late 1960s. Sayer disparagingly depicted them thus in *Wild Country*:

> There they all stood, on the rim of a great natural amphitheatre, looking out across the wilderness; a group of good worthy citizens in Homburg hats and raincoats and pointed town shoes.
>
> "Just a barren wilderness", said one stout alderman to another "and a perfect site for a reservoir", and I think he voiced the opinion of the majority of that particular party. But a minority of those present felt – and said – that he could only have produced that remark out of a totally barren mind.

As Ashbrook suggested, Sayer was equally famous for her cutting letters. She conducted a heated correspondence with Sir Henry Studholme in *The Times* in August 1971 when the Swincombe Reservoir scheme was being revived. He claimed that it made no difference to the Swincombe valley whether it became a reservoir or not, claiming that it would be equally unspoilt and inspiring. Sayer's sharp riposte firmly put Sir

Henry in his place:

> Fortunate Sir Henry Studholme who seems able to persuade himself that a huge artificial dam, roads and associated structures are objects of wild and natural beauty, and that by some modern miracle people are able to walk on water.

Sir Ronald Brockman, chairman of the Dartmoor National Park committee, once even called the police to evict Sayer and some of her friends from the public gallery during a committee meeting in June 1975. She had protested loudly at the meeting at being falsely represented by him to members of the committee while being given no opportunity to reply.

In 1975, Sayer devised a plan to save the rather prosaically named "Area Y" on Shaugh Moor in south-west Dartmoor from being used by a china clay company as a gigantic waste tip. This magnificent stretch of moorland, with its rich palimpsest of ancient monuments, stone rows and circles, was thus saved for posterity.

When she was not fighting to preserve Dartmoor, Sayer was

China clay works, Lee Moor, Dartmoor (Nilfanion/Wikimedia Commons)

also a very talented artist. When bored at meetings she would sometimes sketch perfect likenesses of those round the table with her. In Sayer's meticulous drawing of the parish church of St Pancras in Widecombe-in-the-Moor, the borders represent the inhabitants from 1066 to 1949, and the roundels show local scenes, all intricately intertwined.

Ashbrook adds: "Because she was so outspoken and made many enemies, her human side tended to be overlooked. She was exceptionally warm, kind and humorous with a large and close family (five grandchildren and, at the time of her death, seven great grandchildren) and a multitude of friends whom she welcomed to Cator – where there was always a roaring fire and a good tea." And Ashbrook recounts a charming story which reveals Sayer's love of nature in all its forms:

> One summer evening, when Guy was reading to her in bed as he normally did, a moth flew into her ear and did not fly out again. Unable to budge it, and unable to sleep because of the fluttering torture in her head, she got up and wrote Dartmoor letters all night, including one to the *Telegraph*, so as not to waste time when she couldn't sleep. The next day the doctor flushed out the moth and she was delighted to find it was still alive.

In 1983, Sayer contracted a cancer in her eyelid, and she bravely opted to have her eye removed. "With her black patch, she looked as fearsome as ever," recalled Ashbrook.

In a 1981 essay entitled *Wild landscape: Dartmoor - the influence and inspiration of its past*, Sayer described the unique continuity of history which she experienced on Dartmoor:

> As you approach Dartmoor's heights from the cultivated Devon lowlands the centuries fall away faster than the mileage until finally you arrive in the landscape of the Bronze Age; and sometimes this brings a kind of involuntary recognition that you have been here before – a long time before – and here are your roots, this is

your tribal land.

In 1966, Devon County Alderman Sir Henry Slesser, with whom Sayer had clashed on the National Park committee in 1957, apparently conceded that she was right after all. He wrote a collection of Dartmoor poems called *This Barren Waste*, one of which was about Sayer, the opening lines of which are quoted at the head of this chapter. It concludes:

*To all who would menace the Moor*
*Her responses are drastic but sure -*
*While commercialists fear her*
*The ramblers revere her*
*For she is the shield of the Moor.*

# 10. "I'm Not Going Back"
## Benny Rothman (1911-2002)

As we entered the rocky confines of William Clough, which marks the western limit of Kinder Scout, we raised a red grouse, which clattered into the air sounding its characteristic "Go back, go back, go back" warning cackle.

The face of Benny Rothman, leader of the famous Mass Trespass which took place on this route in 1932, broke into that familiar broad grin. "No, my friend," he smiled warmly, addressing the grouse, "I'm not going back."

It was a walk which I'll always treasure and one which I'll never forget. I was walking the trespass route with Rothman and his wife Lily, both then in their seventies, retracing their steps from over fifty years before. Rothman, five foot three in his size seven boots, was still walking like a train, and I was hard pressed to keep up with him.

We had walked up from the Bowden Bridge quarry where he had been pushed into speaking at the rally which preceded

Benny Rothman at Bowden Bridge (Mike Harding)

the iconic event on Sunday 24 April 1932, after the scheduled speaker had got cold feet and backed out.

The event had been organised by the Lancashire branch of the British Workers' Sports Federation, a Young Communist League (YCL) organisation of which Benny was the branch secretary. It arose after a group of BWSF walkers, including some visitors from London, had been unceremoniously turned off Bleaklow that Easter that year by abusive and threatening gamekeepers. "We decided then and there to prove the point," said Rothman. "If there was enough of us, they couldn't turn us back."

Rothman later described the "inspiring" picture which faced him in the quarry. "There were hundreds of young men and women in their picturesque rambling gear: shorts of every length and colour, flannels and breeches, even overalls, vivid colours and drab khaki (khaki shorts and shirts were fashionable at the time), multi-coloured sweaters and pullovers, army packs and rucksacks of every size and shape."

Rothman's speech delivered from the natural pulpit in the quarry started with a brief outline of the "injustice" of the Enclosure Movement, a history of the failed Access to Mountains legislation since 1884, and the "ruthless" lobbying by landowners which had blocked it. He called for the Mass Trespass to be the start of a campaign to back up the other organisations fighting for access to mountains. "I denied

Benny Rothman addresses the Mass Trespass at Bowden Bridge Quarry on April 24, 1932 (Willow Publishing)

the stories in the Press that said we were hooligans intent on trouble," continued Rothman. "We were not intending to injure or damage anybody or anything. We wanted a peaceful demonstration ramble but we were determined not to be diverted nor stopped."

The story of what happened next is now firmly embedded in rambling folklore. After the speeches, the joyful, arm-in-arm, singing procession of about 400 ramblers set out up the Kinder Road by Nab Brow above the reservoir and into William Clough. Singing was an essential part of rambling in the 1930s, and the revolutionary songs they sang included "The Internationale" and "The Red Flag".

The ramblers were about half-way up William Clough on the Hayfield to Snake Pass public footpath (which had been negotiated by the Peak and Northern Counties Footpaths Association as long ago as 1897), when the trespass actually began. At the pre-arranged signal of three blasts on a whistle, the ramblers started to scramble up the steep slopes of the forbidden ground of Sandy Heys in what was described as an open formation.

A line of between twenty and thirty keepers was lying in wait for them and in the few, undistinguished scuffles which followed one temporary keeper was knocked to the ground, injuring an ankle. Press photographs taken at the time actually show concerned ramblers coming to his assistance.

John Watson was one of the group of gamekeepers waiting on Sandy Heys. He claimed afterwards: "We could hear them cheering and yelling as if they had achieved something, when they had achieved nothing at all. They had only trespassed about fifty yards – they never even got halfway up the clough."

It is true that the trespassers got nowhere near Kinder's elusive summit as is sometimes claimed – but then, few people have. Rothman later agreed that the so-called "victory meeting", when the Hayfield group met up with others from Sheffield who had come by the much more challenging route across Kinder's peaty plateau from Edale, was held near Ashop Head, at least two miles north-west of Kinder's boggy summit. But in the end, the important fact was that they had trespassed in such a public and positive way, rather than how far they had trespassed.

Rothman and the trespassers agreed that they would march back into Hayfield "with their heads held high" and not disperse like a band of criminals. "It was a demonstration for the rights of ordinary people to walk on land stolen from them in earlier times," Rothman was to write later. "We were proud of our effort and we proudly marched back the way we had come."

The police, who had declined the invitation to scramble up Kinder's steep flanks, were waiting in a line across Kinder Road when the trespassers returned. Six ramblers were arrested and charged with various public order offences such as incitement to cause a riotous assembly, but significantly, none were charged with trespass, as it is not, and never has been, a criminal offence.

At their trial at Derby Assizes in July, five defendants were found guilty and sentenced to between two and six months' imprisonment. Rothman received a sentence of four months, but he told me he had spent the time productively learning shorthand, which was to prove useful in later life when he became a trade union representative.

His self-conducted defence at the trial, composed in the darkness of a Leicester prison cell, was a masterpiece of open-air, working-class rhetoric. "We ramblers," he told the court, "after a hard week's work in smoky towns and cities, go out rambling for relaxation, a breath of fresh air, a little sunshine. But we find when we go out that the finest rambling country is closed to us, just because certain individuals wish to shoot for about ten days a year."

But when I walked the route with Rothman in the early 1980s, his memories of that momentous event from half a century before were a little indistinct. As we stopped for our "snap" in the shadow of the last rowan tree in William Clough, he said he couldn't remember exactly where they had left the right-of-way to clash with the gamekeepers. And he reflected that maybe the trespassers should have cooperated more closely with the established ramblers' federations, who were totally opposed to the idea of a mass trespass. "Maybe we could have achieved something more quickly if we had all worked together," he said.

As it was, the official ramblers' federations at the time were totally opposed to the mass trespass, although many members, including such leading lights as Tom Stephenson (see Chapter 6), admitted to regularly trespassing as individuals.

The Manchester federation and others unsuccessfully appealed to the Home Secretary for a remission of the vicious sentences, while the *Manchester Guardian* (as it was then) compared the event to a university student rag, pointing out that people arrested during a riotous student event were not usually sent to prison. Even Bert Ward's (see Chapter 4) Sheffield Clarion Club Handbook of 1933-34 reported that the stiff sentences handed out by the judge "did not bring laurels to the other side".

After he was released from prison later in 1932, Rothman found it very difficult to find work locally, especially as he now had a prison record. He became more closely involved with the Young Communist League, and in supporting a long-running strike by clothing workers in Burnley, East Lancashire. Returning home, he helped to resurrect the Cheetham branch of the YCL, which became one of the largest and most active in the country. This was at the time of the rise of fascism in Germany, Italy and in Britain, where it took the form of Oswald Mosley's infamous "Blackshirts" – the British Union of Fascists.

Rothman helped organise the local opposition to Moseley's BUF in Manchester, which eventually made it impossible for them to hold their rallies there. "At any event they organised we turned up and heckled them, and at one meeting we turned their van over," recalled Rothman. He was arrested once again on another occasion, but the charge was dropped.

Rothman had a lucky escape at a large BUF rally held at Manchester's Free Trade Hall in March 1933, when for once in his life, he actually found himself indebted to a fascist. Fighting had erupted between BUF and anti-fascist supporters, most of whom were members of the YCL. Rothman was on the balcony of the hall when the fighting broke out, when he was manhandled and hurled over the balcony by a burly BUF supporter. Fortunately, he had his fall broken by landing on top of another unsuspecting BUF member in the stalls below, thus escaping what could have been serious injury. He joked afterwards: "It's the only time in my life that I've been grateful for the presence of a fascist!"

At about this time, Rothman finally found work in a car repair works, and joined the Amalgamated Engineering Union (AEU), using the shorthand he had learned in prison to becoming a minutes secretary and eventually being elected as a delegate to the Manchester and Salford Trades Council. He later obtained a job at the Newton Heath aircraft manufacturing factory of AV Roe (AVRO), but was later sacked apparently after the firm discovered he was a communist.

Just before he lost his job at AVRO, Rothman met fellow young communist and union official Lilian Crabtree from Rochdale. She was from a family of thirteen, of whom only eight survived childhood, which had been forced into the workhouse before Lily's birth. She was also a keen walker and trespasser. The couple married at Christmas in 1937 and originally lived in Failsworth. But when their first child, Harry, was born in 1938, they were able to move into the newly-constructed Riddings estate at Timperley in Cheshire. Their second child, Marion, was born there in 1940.

The couple lived in the end semi-detached house in Crofton Avenue, Timperley for nearly sixty years. It was a privilege for me to join Harry and Marion in attending and speaking at a ceremony in 2013 when Trafford Borough Council unveiled a blue plaque on the family home, which paid tribute to Rothman as an "environmental and access campaigner."

As Britain geared up for the inevitable war with Germany, Rothman was finally able to get a job at the engineering giant Metropolitan Vickers at Trafford Park. He was again active in trade union affairs and became a representative of the Works Committee. He volunteered as a driver to fight against Franco in the Spanish Civil War but was turned down, apparently due to his lack of driving experience.

Rothman worked in various other positions until his retirement in 1976, when he once again became involved in the politics of the countryside. In 1982, he became the first secretary of the Kinder and High Peak Advisory Committee, created after the National Trust had purchased the Kinder estate.

Following the threat of water privatisation, Rothman set up the Rivington Pledge Committee, which published an illuminated pledge, painted by his daughter-in-law Anne Berg, warning against the perceived threat to public access to water board lands in 1989.

\*

I first met Rothman at the fiftieth anniversary celebrations of the Mass Trespass at Hayfield in 1982. I was working as a feature writer for the *Birmingham Post & Mail* at the time and was desperate to find a local angle so I could cover the story. To my great relief, I discovered that Rothman's son Harry was a lecturer at Aston University – giving me that all-important local angle.

Rothman became a good friend and was a man who was always on the ball about the latest threats to access to the countryside. He died in January 2002 aged ninety, in Billericay, Essex, where he was being cared for by his daughter Marion. I still miss his infectious, mischievous smile and his wicked sense of humour.

Rothman lived to witness the passing of the Countryside and Rights of Way (CRoW) Act, 2000, which eventually gave walkers the right to roam in open country for which he had fought so long and hard. But it was a source of great regret that he never saw its implementation, significantly initially in the Peak District, in September 2004.

# 11. The Unna of His Day
## Rennie McOwan (1933-2018)

IT'S A STRANGE FACT BUT my twenty-five-year friendship with
the distinguished Scottish access campaigner and writer Rennie
McOwan began with a heated argument conducted in a rigid
inflatable boat speeding up an icy fjord in Arctic Svalbard.

As McOwan and his good friend Hamish Brown compared
the surrounding, snow-clad peaks with those back home in
the Scottish Highlands, the discussion turned to National
Parks for Scotland. As a former National Park employee and
a long-time supporter of the idea, I found myself at odds with
both McOwan and Brown. "There's no need for another level
of bureaucracy in Scotland," insisted McOwan. "Anyway, the
whole of Scotland is good enough to be a National Park and it
should be treated as one."

Yet from that initial disagreement sprang a mutual respect
and lasting friendship which I'll always treasure. I never
needed to mention the fact that Scotland eventually gained
two National Parks (in the Cairngorms and Loch Lomond and
the Trossachs), because McOwan was also a pragmatist whose
undying love of the Scottish hills and their protection for future
generations was ingrained in his very soul.

It would be no exaggeration to say that McOwan was the
Percy Unna of his generation, such was his campaigning zeal for
the freedom of access to the Scottish hills. Unna (see Chapter
5) was a great wilderness campaigner and generous benefactor
to the National Trust for Scotland in the 1930s, who famously
set up a list of rules which McOwan, as a former deputy press
secretary with the NTS, always strenuously upheld. The Unna
Rules were intended to ensure that land which was held on behalf
of the public should be preserved for their use in a "primitive"
condition, without development or active management.

McOwan fell out with the NTS over this principle, notably
in Glencoe, scene of some of Unna's greatest bequests, over the

construction of the footbridge leading to Coire Gabhail (the "Lost Valley"); a proposed visitor centre near the Clachaig Inn; and the incongruous "space ship" visitor centre on the semi-Arctic slopes of Ben Lawers.

As his good friend the late Irvine Butterfield has written, Unna's legacy and ideas became a source of inspiration for McOwan, and he was determined that his message should not go unheeded, feeling that it held a relevance to today and for the future. But McOwan was taken to task for writing about Unna by NTS, who seemed to want to portray him as a reclusive and obsolete individual. Eventually he resigned so that he could write freely as a freelance on matters close to his heart, such as the NTS and access.

*

Ironically, McOwan's great grandfather Donald Ross had been a legendary chief stalker on the Duke of Portland's Caithness estate. Born in Hillfoots, the son of schoolteachers, McOwan was brought up in Menstrie at the foot of the Ochils in "the wee county" of Clackmannanshire. In an article for the Scottish Book Trust in 2000, he recalled his carefree childhood:

> … (I) had a boyhood in which the green grassy hills with their rocky bluffs, the deep-cut, wooded glens, the sharp, cool scents of running burns, and the recesses of the woods played a prominent part.
>
> Our playground was a hill called Craigomas, another called Dumyat, Menstrie Glen and its wood. Our heritage was a Pictish fort, abandoned mine borings, which we treated as caves, and stories of witches, faeries and clans.

It was on Dumyat that the young McOwan had his first encounter with a recalcitrant landowner, who enquired as to where he thought he and his companion were going. For the first time, McOwan wondered: "Who has the right to deny

McOwan's childhood playground: Dumyat in the Ochils
(Adrianmckie/Wikimedia Commons)

access to the hills?" That opinion was confirmed on a Menstrie scout group trip to the Blackmount Estate, when he recalled the burning feeling of injustice after a meeting with a deer stalker, who suggested that the scouts should assist him by taking a route off the hill of his choosing.

McOwan excelled at History and English at school, paving the way for his distinguished later career in journalism and historical literature. There were no diplomas to be had in those days, and an apprenticeship was considered to be the best way forward for a bright lad like McOwan. He started work as a trainee cub reporter with the *Stirling Journal* covering the traditional fare of a local newspaperman in those days – "hatches, matches and dispatches" (i.e. births, marriages and deaths). He moved on to *The Scotsman* as a sub-editor and became Scottish Desk Editor at the tender age of twenty-three. McOwan later regularly contributed to many Scottish newspapers and magazines, notably *The Scotsman*, *Scotland on Sunday* and the *Scots Magazine*. He was the founder of The Scotsman Mountaineering Club, now the Ptarmigan Hillwalking and Mountaineering Club of Edinburgh, in 1958.

# WALKING CLASS HEROES

By the 1990s, McOwan's reputation as a prolific and established journalist led him to go freelance and to join the movement which was campaigning for land reform in Scotland. He was appalled to find out that the great Scottish mountaineer and author Bill Murray had resigned from the Countryside Commission for Scotland and the NTS when he learned that there were reports of rangers advising visitors that there was no access without permission, because the right of access lay with the owners. McOwan realised that the true nature of the traditional *de facto* rights of access to the Scottish hills had never been fully explained nor understood, and that there was an urgent need to redress this situation. Initially he seemed to be a lone voice, with both the Scottish Mountaineering Council (SMC) and the Scottish Rights of Way Society seemingly disinclined to criticise the landowning fraternity and content with the existing rights of way network.

McOwan later became president of Ramblers Scotland, appropriately in the year that the Scottish Parliament passed what is widely regarded as some of the finest access legislation in the world with the Land Reform Act (Scotland), 2003. And McOwan played a key and influential role in getting that legislation onto the Statute Book.

The meaningless Letterewe Accord had been negotiated by SMC and an Access Forum was set up by the Countryside Commission for Scotland, which astonishingly excluded any representatives of the outdoor community, such as the SMC and the Ramblers. Aided by what he called the "acute legal mind" of Alan Blackshaw, president of the British Mountaineering Council, McOwan ensured that access legislation was put firmly on the agenda of the Scottish Parliament. And he questioned every clause and paragraph of the proposed Land Reform Bill as it went through every stage at Holyrood.

At one point, the farcical suggestion was made that people should be off the hill before dark, to which McOwan was moved to evoke the spirit of the renowned Scottish singer and comedian Harry Lauder: "Since when has 'roamin' in the gloamin'" been an offence?" he enquired.

Irving Butterfield claimed that McOwan's finest hour was when he was invited to address the Landowners' Federation at the launch of the temporary Access Concordat in 1996, which preceded the 2003 legislation. It was at this meeting that McOwan sensed that at long last, "things were going our way." One observer commented that McOwan had "read them the Riot Act" and his crucial address was described by the chair, *Mastermind* host and TV historian Magnus Magnusson, as "statesman-like".

McOwan was the prolific author of more than fifteen mainly historical and children's books, and his *Light on Dumyat* (1982), an adventure involving a group of youngsters called The Clan and set on the 1,375-foot western rampart of his native Ochils, was a particular favourite. One reviewer sagely commented that McOwan's Clan "could outwit Enid Blyton's Famous Five any day of the week."

In 1996, McOwan was awarded an honorary doctorate by Stirling University, where he lectured in film and media studies, for his contribution to Scottish literature and culture. He was awarded the Provost of Stirling's Civic Award for Arts and Culture, and in 1992, he was the founder of the Friends of the Ochils.

McOwan was presented with the Outdoor Writers Guild's coveted Golden Eagle award at its annual dinner at Harrogate in 1997 for his services to Scottish culture and access

Rennie McOwan in Svalbard
(John Cleare/Mountain Camera)

campaigning. Always the proud Scot, he naturally enough turned up in a kilt in the McOwan tartan. Typically, in his acceptance speech, McOwan appealed for the Guild to set up a working group to look into the whole question of access to the countryside of Britain.

To his lasting credit, McOwan always took a keen interest in introducing young people to the hills and regularly visited schools and colleges as a lecturer under the Scottish Arts Council's "Writers in Schools" and "Writers in Public" schemes, and also in the Film and Media Studies Department at Stirling University.

Another thing I shared with McOwan was his choice of his favourite book as a child, Kenneth Grahame's *The Wind in the Willows* (1908). He claimed it was the book he wished he'd written and added: "It was allegedly meant solely for children (who of course love it), but it is really a book for adults too. To this day if I see the line of a far-off wood, I think of The Wild Wood and the terrified Mole." He explained: "When my own children were primary school age we lived in cities and their outdoor world was mainly that of the public park. I began to tell them adventure stories based on my outdoor boyhood, some true, some made up." The result was probably McOwan's most famous children's book, *Light on Dumyat*, which was very well received and has been used as an educational resource in countless Scottish schools, in addition to countries as far away as the USA and Australia.

McOwan lived in Stirling in the shadow of the Ochils with Agnes, his loving wife of over fifty years, whom he met when she was at teacher training college in Edinburgh in 1957. At one time, Agnes was in charge of a mobile school which taught travellers' children. McOwan was a keen football fan and a long-suffering and life-long supporter of Alloa Athletic – nicknamed "the Wasps" after their yellow and black hooped shirts. In later years he suffered from debilitating Parkinson's disease, and his increasing ill health and inability to walk robbed him of his greatest joy of striding the hills, especially his home ground of the Ochils. He died at the age of eighty-five in 2018.

The couple had four children: Lesley Andrews, who runs Rowan Tree Publishing (which has re-published some of her father's children's books); Michael, who lives with his family in Tasmania; Tom and Niall. The couple had five grandchildren.

Hillgoers throughout Scotland and beyond owe an enormous debt of gratitude to the kindly and generous Rennie McOwan, who fought so long and hard so that they could enjoy the freedom of the hills we all enjoy today.

# 12: Creator of the "People's Path"

## Colin Speakman (1941-)

FOR SOMEONE SO CLOSELY ASSOCIATED with the Yorkshire Dales, it comes as something of a surprise to learn that Colin Speakman – author, poet and co-creator of Dales Rail and the Dales Way – was born on "t'other" side of the Pennines in industrial Lancashire.

Speakman came into this world in 1941 at Higher Broughton and was brought up in a terraced house with no electricity and an outside toilet in Pendleton, Salford. He first went to school at the North Grecian Street Primary School, and after passing his 11-plus, to Salford Grammar School.

"Both my parents were keen cyclists," he says. "My Mum was a nursery class teacher, and Dad joined the RAF without any formal training or skills but became a senior mechanic, working on Avro Lancaster bombers and training apprentices. But he was a late developer, and after doing some garage work, he became a technician at Manchester Technical College (later the Manchester Institute of Technology) and worked on some high-profile projects."

So where did his love of the Yorkshire Dales originate? "I fell in love with the Yorkshire Dales when I was reading English at Leeds University between 1959 and 1962," Speakman explains. "That was also where I met my wife of fifty-seven years, Fleur. We found we shared a passion for literature, music – especially opera – and the Yorkshire Dales."

Among the greatest early influences on Speakman as he grew to love the Dales were the great Dales historian and industrial archaeologist Dr Arthur Raistrick, and the access campaigner and creator of the Pennine Way, Tom Stephenson (see Chapter 6), both of whom he came to know as friends. Other Dales people whom the young Speakman knew and respected were his good friend the social historian and rambler David Rubinstein; the celebrated Dales authors and historians Marie Hartley and Joan Ingilby; and the legendary Dalesman Kit Calvert of Hawes, the so-called "saviour" of Wensleydale cheese.

After finishing university in 1962, Speakman spent a year in teacher training at the London University Institute of Education. But he returned to Yorkshire the following year, when he married Fleur and taught English at Bingley Grammar School between 1963 and 1967; at Lawnswood High School, Leeds, between 1967 and 1969; and English and Education at the James Graham College of Education, Leeds, from 1971 to 1975. By this time, Speakman was exploring the Dales on foot and by bike at every opportunity, mostly at weekends. He was Access Secretary for the West Riding Ramblers between 1967 and 1989, and Area Secretary between 1969 and 1975. He also became a member of the Bowland Access Committee, which was then trying to gain greater access for walkers from one of the most intransigent of landowners, the Duke of Westminster, during the 1960s and 1970s. As he became increasingly involved in the national politics of walking and access to the countryside, Speakman served on the National Executive Committee of the Ramblers' Association between 1971 and 1975.

*

His first book, appropriately titled *Walking in the Yorkshire Dales*, was published by Robert Hale in 1967. In it, he expressed his belief that the only way to fully share the experience of the Dales landscape was on foot.

> ... only if you have time to be absorbed into a landscape, to note its many quiet changes of mood and feeling, to use your other senses so betrayed by modern civilisation – your sense of touch, smell, of sound, even of taste – can you begin to understand what the

Dales are all about. Most of us who live in drab towns or suburbs can only escape briefly into the landscape of our dreams. Those moments are precious to us; we must enjoy them to the full.

The car, he wrote, was both the "curse and blessing of our civilisation". And he claimed it was only when we could persuade ourselves to leave the comfort of our vehicle and walk that we could enter a different mode of being.

The rhythm of your own muscles determines your speed of perception. You are made aware of the physical shape of the land – a valley, a hillock, a mound, a crag. You know again the feel of the wind in your face, the fresh smell of earth, the acid tang of oak woods; the sound of becks boiling after rain, the dissonant bleat of sheep on the fellside, the hauntingly sad call of a curlew circling above you.

The Dales Way above Conistone Dib (Chris Heaton/Wikimedia Commons)

Perhaps Speakman's greatest and most lasting legacy will be the eighty-mile Dales Way long-distance path which links the Yorkshire Dales National Park with the Lake District National Park via Wharfedale. Conceived jointly with West Riding Ramblers' footpath secretary Tom Wilcock, this superb route was the first major lowland long-distance trail when it opened in 1969. Starting at the market town of Ilkley, it follows the banks of the River Wharfe, passing the romantic ruins of Bolton Abbey before crossing the wild moorland of Cam Fell and descending into Dentdale and passing Sedbergh and the Crook o'Lune. It then meanders through the foothills of the Lakes to reach Bowness, on the shores of England's largest lake, Windermere.

"The Dales Way was inspired by Tom Stephenson's Pennine Way," admits Speakman. "But this magnificent traverse of the Yorkshire Dales is very different from the wild and rugged Pennine Way, as it's mostly a riverside walk through sheltered dales, with plenty of places to stay at and get refreshment... By encouraging people to walk the Dales Way, we hoped to create awareness of the remarkable heritage of Definitive Rights of Way, newly established and available for everyone, as well as the two National Parks... It was truly the People's Path."

Speakman's *Dales Way* guide, first published in 1970, is now in its eleventh edition and still in print. It has inspired many other guides to this popular route as well as linking footpath routes to the towns of Leeds, Bradford and Harrogate. He has been chair of the Dales Way Association since 1993.

Speakman joined the staff of the Yorkshire Dales National Park authority in 1975 as Field Services Officer, concerned principally with the promotion of public transport to and from the Dales. Later as a Principal Officer, he established the groundbreaking Dales Rail project, which used the existing rail network to transport people from the surrounding towns and cities into the Dales, leaving their cars behind, while at the same time carrying Dalesfolk to the towns to do their shopping. He also managed the negotiation of access agreements for the Park, and he ensured that the Barden Fell Access Agreement, agreed with the Chatsworth

Estate under the provisions of the 1949 National Parks and Access to the Countryside Act, was a great success.

He left the National Park staff in 1980, and between 1983 and 1984 was appointed as a Secretary of State nominee to the National Park Committee. Speakman founded the Yorkshire Dales Society – now Friends of the Dales – support group in 1981, acting as secretary and vice chair, and later becoming chair and now a vice-president of the society. Continuing his passion for the promotion of public transport, Speakman joined the West Yorkshire Public Transport Executive in 1980 as Recreation Transport Officer and was County Tourism Officer for West Yorkshire County Council for a short spell between 1983 and 1984.

Speakman set up his own transport consultancy, Transport for Leisure, in 1984. This specialist consultancy was dedicated to improving and developing public transport access to the countryside, walking and cycling and it did pioneering work in nearly all the UK National Parks. He later became an adviser to the Countryside Commission and the Countryside Council for Wales, and also worked in mainland Europe – including East Germany, Hungary, Slovakia and Poland.

Among the many awards and honours Speakman has won is an Honorary Doctorate of Letters from Bradford University in 1987, *The Dalesman* Lifetime Achievement Award in 2007 and the Sheila McKechnie Foundation National Transport Campaigner award in 2015 for his work on Dales Rail and DalesBus.

DalesBus is a community interest company set up by Speakman in 2007 which manages a network of integrated bus services in the Yorkshire Dales National Park and the Forest of Bowland and Nidderdale Areas of Outstanding Natural Beauty (AONBs), linking them to the surrounding cities.

Speakman is also a member of Gritstone, Britain's first writers' publishing co-operative, and the author or co-author of about sixty books, including four volumes of poetry. "Poetry matters hugely to me," he admits, "and my own poetry is the work I value most."

Speakman's children have followed in their father's conservation footsteps. Daughter Lydia, who was born in 1967, is now a senior manager with Natural England in charge of National Nature Reserves (NNRs) in the North East of England. His son Dorian, born in 1970, is equally passionate about climate and ecology and works for Leeds City Council as part of its flood alleviation team. His wife Kasia is a senior officer with Leeds City Council on cycling and access issues.

On the subject of access to the countryside, Speakman believes this country should follow the Swedish or German model of *Allemansrätten* ("everyman's right"). "I believe we should have claimed full access rights on all our open fells until challenged, then used the legal powers of agreement as per 1949 Access to the Countryside Act," he says.

The Countryside and Rights of Way Act of 2000 increased the area of open country where the public had a legal right of access in the Yorkshire Dales from 4 per cent to a massive 62 per cent – a total of 390 square miles. "This was the most dramatic change to access availability on open land in any National Park in the United Kingdom," claims Speakman.

Colin Speakman (Ramblers)

In his sixtieth anniversary book on the Yorkshire Dales National Park, Speakman expresses his view that compared with the old unregulated *de facto* access, CRoW has actually brought in a greater degree of control and regulation. "In truth, most walkers don't wish to walk far from a clear path or track," he remarks. "The demand among walkers to walk the wild paces is small. But the right to do so if they wish is perhaps deeply symbolic, a cherished freedom... The fears of landowners about 'hordes' of walkers tramping the heather, scaring the grouse chicks, knocking down walls and leaving huge amounts of litter and damage were largely unfounded."

But he adds: "The trade off on removing rights of way if not recorded by 2026 is deplorable. I believe that our unique rights of way network to be even more important than access to open country."

# 13: Howard's Way
## Terry Howard (1945-)

**FIRST APPEARANCES CAN BE DECEPTIVE.** When I first met Terry Howard, the redoubtable Sheffield access campaigner, nearly twenty years ago, I was immediately reminded of Rasputin, the Russian Tsarist mystic and holy man. He had shoulder-length greying hair and a luxuriant beard which reached down to his chest.

But I soon learned that this fearsome presence belied a gentle, highly intelligent man, totally in love with the moors which form the so-called "Golden Frame" and mark the western boundary of the Steel City.

Howard had been introduced to the hills bordering the city when his steelworker father Henry took him and his younger brother John on regular expeditions. They visited places like Greno Woods, Wharncliffe Crags and Ecclesfield, using their meths stove and a battered old coffee pot for picnics, and pretending they were looking for "treasure". It is a fond memory which has always stayed with Howard. "It was on one of these expeditions to a local moor where I think I first developed my lasting feeling of injustice of not being able to walk freely on the moors," he recalls.

> There was a mound in the distance with something on the top of it which caught our interest. Knowing it was a "private" moor, we gingerly climbed over the wall and crept along, so as not to be seen and sent back, or worse, by the gamekeeper. As we got close to it, we looked up and saw a sign which said, "Private Keep Out". I'd never forget it, and that sense of injustice has always stayed with me.

Howard was born at Manor Top, Sheffield, and brought up on the Parsons Cross council estate in the north of the city. At the age of ten, in what he still regards as a seminal moment in his life, Howard joined the Woodcraft Folk, a socialist organisation founded in London in 1924 by nineteen-year-old Leslie Paul, which introduced thousands of young people to the outdoors. Thereafter he spent every summer weekend rambling, youth hostelling, bivouacking and camping in the countryside around Sheffield.

"One of my Woodcraft leaders, Basil Rawson (or Brown Eagle as we knew him) would tell us keen Woodcrafters about the Kinder and Abbey Brook mass trespasses of 1932, and how and why people such as us were not allowed to go onto those then forbidden moorlands," he recalls. "Those events gave a sense of inspiration and challenge to us youngsters... I think it particularly stuck with me because of the injustice for people such as my Dad, who had spent many years fighting a war for his country, yet on his return, had to creep furtively over the moors just to admire the view."

Howard later became a Woodcraft leader himself, taking kids from the city on rambles and camping in the countryside, as indeed he still does. "But always in the back of my mind was the injustice of not being able to wander freely over all the moorlands to the west of Sheffield."

Later, with his brother John, Howard set out to explore these forbidden moorlands. On one memorable occasion, they set out from Parsons Cross to walk to the remote 1,793-foot summit of Margery Hill on the moors above Broomhead, simply because it shared their mother's name. They had tried to reach it once before as youngsters, but then, as Howard admits, "it was a step too far" for their young legs.

Howard recounts the story of that expedition as if it were yesterday. "Leaving the Ewden Valley behind, we walked along the Dukes Road in worsening weather conditions," he recalls. "Rain turned to snow and by the time we reached Flint Hill it was snowing heavily. Not to be deterred I made a compass bearing for Margery Hill, which meant crossing the wide, featureless expanse of Broomhead Moor.

"By this time the snow had deepened to a metre in places. We slipped, tripped, fell into peat groughs but eventually we reached Margery Hill. By this time, the snow had turned into an icy blizzard, with all the rocks covered in thick ice. We needed to descend rapidly into the Derwent Valley, which we did. But within a very short distance, we had left the blizzard behind and we were walking through pleasant heather and grass."

Kinder Scout, at 2,088 feet the highest summit in the Peak District, was the ultimate challenge to Howard and his friends. "There were stories of people being lost and dying up there in atrocious weather conditions. There were bogs to fall into, rapid changes in weather conditions to be aware of, and nowhere to shelter."

So it was with some trepidation that they set out for Kinder on their first encounter with the iconic mountain. "We walked up Grindsbrook then took a stream leading on to the top. We scrambled and climbed up the waterfalls with water running up our sleeves and getting fairly wet. We eventually reached the top and felt immensely elated and exhilarated on 'conquering' Kinder – and our fears. It was a clear day, and you could see for miles over the plateau. We were on top of the world."

By this time, Howard had left Yew Lane Secondary School with two O-Levels to his name and started work first as a TV salesman and taking other similar "boring" jobs. He then found more suitable employment as a forestry worker and part-time dam keeper for the water authority. He married his wife June Whitehead at Ecclesfield Church in 1966, and the couple have three children, two girls and a boy. Howard continues: "It was while I was working as a dam keeper that I realised how much I was learning about the world around me, and I thought I shouldn't keep this to myself and needed to share it with others, particularly children."

He studied hard at night school and eventually qualified as a teacher at Lady Mabel College, in the stately surroundings of the Palladian-style Wentworth Woodhouse, near Barnsley. Howard taught environmental studies at a Melton Mowbray school in Leicestershire for a few years where once again he took children out into the countryside, particularly to the Peak District. All the time, though, he was missing the moors of his childhood and he eventually returned to Sheffield as a supply teacher. Even then he often found himself asking "What am I doing here?" and he eventually started working for himself as a landscape gardener.

It was shortly after returning to Sheffield from Melton Mowbray that Howard became involved in the "right to roam" campaign. "Just before the fiftieth Anniversary of the Kinder Mass Trespass in 1982," he recalls, "a letter in a local newspaper asked what was being done about access in the Peak District, as there was still over 50 per cent of the moorlands in the Peak District without public access. The challenge had been made."

A trespass walk was organised and to the surprise of Howard and the organisers, over 200 people turned out. Another walk was organised to mark the fiftieth anniversary celebrations in Hayfield. "I remember going over Jacob's Ladder and down to Bowden Bridge and joining the gathered mass of people," says Howard. "I, along with others from Sheffield, was inspired by the words of Benny Rothman (see Chapter 10) who had said: 'We must carry on where we left off in 1932.'"

Back in Sheffield Howard and others founded the Sheffield Campaign for Access to Moorland (SCAM) in 1982. This was followed by a regular programme of trespass walks over all the then-off-limits moorlands. In 1988, the group also produced a booklet entitled *Freedom of the Moors*, a walking guide in which every route described was a deliberate trespass.

As an outdoor writer, I desperately wanted to review this guide, since I considered it was in the best traditions of Peak District trespassing. But at the time I was Head of Information Services for the Peak District National Park, and I knew I would be in trouble if a review was seen coming from an officer of the National Park authority. So for the first time in my journalist career, I used a *nom de plume*, using my middle names to create a fictional reviewer called "George Samuels".

SCAM continued to trespass and vigorously campaign to influence the Ramblers' Association to be more proactive on access. Few groups in the country did more than SCAM to give the public the right to roam that is now enjoyed on mountains and moorlands, and I was proud to be a member. Regular lobbying activities and meetings were held by the group with the Peak District National Park Authority to negotiate more Access Agreements or Orders on the National Park's moorlands.

Of course, the Holy Grail was finally achieved with the passing of the Countryside and Rights of Way Act in 2000. Howard recalls the feeling of achievement he felt at this partial, if not final, victory:

> It was in November 1999 when we stood on the edge of the forbidden Midhope moors with transistor radios in hand waiting for 11 o'clock to hear what was to be in the Queen's Speech. It was there – the Blair government was to introduce the "Right to Roam" legislation. Bottles of champagne emerged from rucksacks, and a big cheer went up. It was a celebration never to be forgotten.

But Howard and every other rambler had to wait until September 2004 for their "first footing" on the newly-freed Access Land. He reflected: "It was almost an anti-climax after all those years of campaigning and trespassing to raise the profile of the right to roam: "I walked through the new access gate, stopped, looked around, there was no one watching me, but the 'no access' signs had gone. I was free at last. But I couldn't help thinking of all those past access campaigners who had gone and never saw this day for which they long since campaigned – GHB Ward, Benny Rothman, Tom Stephenson, and so many others."

Terry Howard (The Ramblers)

Howard became a founding, and the longest serving, member of the first Local Access Forum in the country, set up under the CRoW Act to review and advise footpath authorities on improvements to public access to the countryside, when he joined the Peak District LAF in 2000. He later became chairman of the Sheffield LAF and has also served as chairman and secretary of the South Yorkshire and North East Derbyshire branch of the Ramblers.

Few people have as much love for and knowledge of the Peak District moors as Terry Howard. To illustrate this abiding passion, on the celebrations of tenth anniversary of the implementation of the CRoW Act at Longshaw in 2014, he recounted an incident which occurred when he was walking across Broomhead Moor, exploring its many fascinating features.

> I looked down and in front of me between two rocks was a flint arrowhead – my first find of a prehistoric artefact. As I picked it up all sorts of thoughts came into my head. Perhaps I was the first person to have touched this in four thousand years, after whoever had lost it. I felt there was some kind of communication between us two hunters. What was that person like? What language did they speak? What did they say on realising they had shot and lost this arrow?
>
> I imagined that they must have said something like: "It took me two days to make this arrowhead – and now I've bloody lost it!" And it was probably said in a broad South Yorkshire accent.

Howard also recalled a night out on Back Tor, Derwent Edge. This was the place where one his own heroes, the Sheffield journalist John Derry, had claimed that "the spirit of the moors has his throne". Howard said: "I settled down for the night in a rock shelter when it started to rain. I soon heard the trickling of water above me, then behind me, then into my sleeping bag. The rest of the night was spent sat up and waiting for morning... At first light I came out of the shelter, somewhat damp, and stood on top of a rock. The sun arose and its first warming rays hit my body. My arms outstretched to feel the full effect of the sun and to welcome the day. The moors below lit up and seemed to be clothed in green and brown velvet."

Howard has led hundreds of walks for people of all ages and abilities in all terrains, including urban areas, to explore, to understand and to enjoy their surroundings. For him, a walk on the moors was, and still is, "a journey of adventure, excitement, learning, challenge and exhilaration, with a feeling of a sense of place, belonging, ownership and commitment."

# 14: Legging It
## Rodney Legg (1947-2011)

**WHAT CAN YOU SAY ABOUT** a man who regularly attended posh National Trust council meetings straight from a walk, in muddy trainers and carrying wire cutters? Rodney Legg's uninhibited and often outrageous contributions enlivened many a stuffy meeting, and he could certainly always be relied on to cut to the chase.

Legg was a prolific author and indefatigable access and environmental campaigner, variously described as "the arch-scourge of politicians, governments, the military and the Establishment in general" and also as "a perfect pest". Equally, the *Guardian* described him as a "one-man Dorset cultural institution", and his 125 books (he described them as his "six feet of books") made a valuable cultural and historic contribution to the literature of the South West of England.

While those descriptions go some way towards describing this larger-than-life character, Legg was much more than that. He was a genuine force of nature whose mere presence at a meeting would make Establishment bureaucrats quake.

Although he may have made a few enemies along the way, Legg changed the way the National Trust was run and allowed access to its properties: he tried (unsuccessfully) to open up the abandoned village of Tyneham in the Lulworth Ranges; he was instrumental

Rodney Legg in typical pose
(Halsgrove Publishing)

in acquiring and then managing Steep Holm in the Bristol Channel as a memorial to his friend, the broadcaster and nature writer Kenneth Allsop: and he ran Britain's oldest conservation charity, the Open Spaces Society, for twenty-five years.

Legg was born the second son of Ted (a cobbler) and Gladys in April 1947 in Easter Road, Bournemouth, after one of the longest and coldest winters on record. He describes his childhood with his elder brother Barrie as "feral" in his autobiography. "In my free time I was always in perpetual motion. It ran in the family as sunny Sundays were always outdoors, to the coast and the countryside, for me to tick off ancient monuments and the parents to enjoy a picnic."

An 11-plus failure, he left Winton Secondary School in 1963 at sixteen with just five O-Levels to his name ("the same as the Prince of Wales," as he liked to remind people). This was just enough to qualify him as a trainee journalist on the *Basildon Standard* in Essex, where he worked after spending six months as a clerk in the unlikely surroundings of the former Atomic Energy Establishment on Winfrith Heath in his native Dorset.

Among Legg's colleagues during his four years as a cub reporter in the "overspill" New Town of Basildon, was Don McPhee, later to become an award-winning and much-respected photographer with the *Guardian*. It was in Basildon that Legg learned journalism the hard way, covering road accidents, arson, murders, sex and suicides among the transplanted East End community. "I uncaringly floated on the adrenaline surge of constantly unfolding events. I still miss the excitement," he was to write later.

Somewhat surprisingly to those who knew him in later life, Legg was then caught up with the reactionary, right-wing pressure group, the League of Empire Loyalists. Typically, he made a nuisance of himself around the country by heckling and interrupting many speeches by the leading politicians of the time, including the former Colonial Secretary Iain MacLeod, Angus Maude, later to become Paymaster General, Randolph Churchill and even the Prime Minister Harold Macmillan.

After a spell working in London on magazines published by Michael Heseltine's Haymarket Press, Legg returned to his native Dorset with his first partner, Colin Graham. He discovered that the Ministry of Defence had reneged on its long-standing agreement to allow the villagers of Tyneham to return to their homes after they had been evicted to allow military training during the war. Frustrated by the forelock-tugging, Establishment-backing attitude of other magazines, Legg founded his own entitled *Dorset: The County Magazine* (now *Dorset Life*) partly to fight the unwanted MoD occupation.

With others he formed the Tyneham Action Group, and in a stirring speech delivered at the inaugural meeting he declared: "Tyneham is devastated. Its cottages and farms are smashed by shellfire... So a simple return and a genuine honouring of the pledge is no longer possible." Instead, he urged the creation of a new coastal path. "One answer must be to advocate that this superb stretch of five miles of the finest British coastline – from Lulworth Cove to Kimmeridge – is given to the National Trust. People have a right to visit it." The Dorset Coast Path, now part of the 630-mile South West Coast Path, was opened in 1974 and in its first official guide, Legg's good friend Brian Jackman paid tribute to him as "an inexhaustible fund of knowledge on every imaginable aspect of Dorset" and "a tireless champion of walkers' rights".

By the time the Tyneham Action Group wound up in 1974, Legg had already moved on to other campaigns, including interventions to save Powerstock Common from clear-felling and coniferous plantation by the Forestry Commission. It was during this campaign that Legg first met and befriended the journalist, broadcaster and nature writer Kenneth Allsop, who lived in an old mill near Bridport. After Allsop tragically took his own life in 1973, Legg, Jackman, author John Fowles, composer Andrew Lloyd Webber and others decided to find somewhere which could be a living memorial to Allsop.

Legg was enlisted to find that special place and, after much argument and negotiation, it was agreed that the unpopulated fifty-acre rocky island of Steep Holm marooned out in the Bristol Channel was the ideal location.

Cliffs at South Landing, Steep Holm (alifetimeofislands.blogspot.com)

Steep Holm is about six miles offshore from the seaside resort of Weston-super-Mare in Somerset and enjoys fantastic views of the Somerset and Welsh coasts. The island has probably been occupied as far back as the Stone Age, before rising sea levels cut it off from the mainland, and in addition to being a haven for wildlife, it has a long and interesting human history. The Vikings – the word "holm" comes from the Old Norse *holmr* meaning small island – probably used it as a base from which to raid the mainland. The Augustinian Priory of St Michael was established there in 1150. Warreners bred rabbits for their meat and for their fur to trim the robes of noblemen. In the eighteenth century, Steep Holm was the main supplier to Bristol Fish Market and its fisheries landed half a ton of fish every day. A hotel and inn built in the 1800s provided illicit liquor for thirsty sailors.

Recognising its strategic position commanding the Bristol Channel, the Victorians fortified the island, and six gun emplacements, complete with cannon, remain largely intact. Massive gun batteries were also built during the Second World War, along with searchlight posts and rocket launch sites.

Steep Holm is now a nature reserve, a bird sanctuary and a Site of Special Scientific Interest (SSSI) due to its rare plants, including the crimson-flowered Mediterranean peony and an original stock of wild leeks, both probably introduced by those Augustinian monks. And most gratifyingly, Allsop's favourite bird, the mercenary peregrine falcon, has returned to its precipitous northern cliffs.

Legg was Steep Holm's enthusiastic and tireless warden for a quarter of a century, transporting thousands of visitors from the mainland to explore the fascinating little island and doing the hard, physical labour of re-building endless miles of walls which had fallen into disrepair himself. More controversially, he introduced hedgehogs and muntjac deer to the island.

Legg took over the chairmanship of the Open Spaces Society in 1989 and, working with its energetic new general secretary Kate Ashbrook (see Chapter 18), re-invigorated a fusty old organisation into a no-holds-barred campaigning body.

He started as he meant to go on with an attack on the "moorland mafia" of the grouse shooting landlords, who were pressuring the Thatcher government to abandon its commitment to provide access to registered commons. He announced: "I'm gunning for the powerful moorland mafia of earls, marquises and baronets who are trying to stop the commons being protected. There are not very many of them but they have been running England for 1,000 years. The Government had a manifesto pledge at the last election to give public access to all common land."

Legg joined the ruling council of the National Trust, which the Open Spaces Society (then the Commons Preservation Society) had helped to form, in 1990, and almost immediately began to ruffle feathers in a long and heated debate over the licensing of hunting on Trust land. After the debate, Trust chair Dame Jennifer Jenkins, wife of Labour politician Roy Jenkins, apparently strode over to him and announced: "Our meetings are never lengthy, contentious or confrontational!" That was wishful thinking with Rodney Legg as a member...

Legg duly made a damning indictment of the Trust for illegally blacking public footpaths, enclosing common land and keeping secret its ownership of properties, including Max Gate in Dorchester, former home of Thomas Hardy. He told the *Guardian* that the organisation fell short of its founders' ideals as a landowner and that even the Ministry of Defence was often a better guardian of the natural landscape. The paper's cartoonist David Austin portrayed a couple looking up at a "NT" sign and saying: "I think it stands for 'No Trespassing'." Legg also told the journal *Rural Socialism*: "From being an egalitarian access organisation promoting the public good, the Trust has become an elitist club of art connoisseurs," who protected "a prime collection of dinosaurs".

A year before the Trust's much-heralded centenary in 1995, Legg published his own account of its history, pointing out that two of its founders – Octavia Hill (see Chapter 2) and Robert Hunter – were his predecessors in the Commons Preservation Society (later the Open Spaces Society). Calling for a crusade to make the Trust more representative, he described the current membership as "almost entirely white, aged and middle class". Legg called for better and more public access to Trust properties, including the adoption of a Swedish-style *Allemansrätten* freedom to roam policy on all Trust-owned farmland and open country.

Representing the Trust at a Buckingham Palace garden party in 1995, he cheekily told the Queen that he regularly invoked her name when asked what he was doing on a public footpath equipped with wire-clipping secateurs. He said his stock reply was: "Trying to proceed along the Queen's highway." Her Majesty, apparently, *was* amused.

Among the other campaigns that Legg was involved in during his time on the National Trust council were the row over banning hunting on Trust land and the move against the tradition of the council of coming to a consensus rather than taking a vote. "When I used to vote I was the only one who did so but I still lost the vote," he said. "We should at least have a vote now on whether or not to have voting."

## WALKING CLASS HEROES

In January 2007, Legg's standing as an Open Spaces Society nominee came under serious threat, and the internal appointments committee proposed its deletion. In what the new secretary general Fiona Reynolds (see Chapter 19) claimed afterwards was "Rodney's finest hour", he spelt out in an emotional speech how the society had actually been responsible for the setting up of the Trust in the first place.

In his retiring speech in November 2009, Legg told members that the Trust owned 1,000 square miles of England – the size of an old English county – and that it must do everything in its power to avoid the Health and Safety anti-risk culture. "Most counties contain their share of feudal estates that have spent the past 500 years keeping the public out," he said. "Much of this green and pleasant land is now being put behind new money fences, gates, walls and closed-circuit television cameras that give the message 'Keep Out' and 'Go Away'. NT does not stand for No Trespassing," he added, referring to David Austen's *Guardian* cartoon. "We must continue to heighten our risk profile by inviting people to step on our land, fall into our lakes and rivers, and get clobbered by wind-borne debris from our six to twelve million 'killer' trees." He praised the new chairman, journalist and author Simon Jenkins, for "telling it as it is." "… if the nation wants the equivalent of an open house countryside," he concluded, "then it will have to accept the statistics that come with it. Otherwise they will restrict the landscape to visual access only."

Legg always believed that people should have "an access passport" to all land and was delighted when the Countryside and Rights of Way Act of 2000 enabled him to claim 640 acres of new access land in Dorset and Somerset.

Legg was a prolific author, antiquarian and collector of books about Dorset on subjects which ranged from prehistory (he had a special fascination with the enigmatic bulging-eyed Celtic heads) and the Romans to the Second World War. He was also a frequent contributor to national newspapers and magazines. Towards the end of his life he lived with his companion Di Hooley and his cherished cat whom he named

Salman Legg. In 2010 he was diagnosed with heart disease and pancreatic cancer, which frustratingly severely limited his walking and other outdoor activities. Legg died from cancer at the age of sixty-four in July 2011.

# 15: On and Off the Rocks
## Jim Perrin (1947-)

**AS A CHILD BROUGHT UP** in the closely packed, smog racked terraces of industrial Manchester, Jim Perrin, for many Britain's finest outdoor writer and journalist, would often gaze longingly up to the distant line of moors which demarcate the eastern skyline of the city. "I remember standing as a child in one or other of the city's scuffed green spaces – Seymour or St George's Park, or Platt Fields – which allow the horizon to rear up beyond the hemming streets and seeing the hills there, bluey-green, far away, mysteriously desirable, like the realisation of a hymn or a dream," he fondly recalls.

It was inevitable that Perrin would find his way to those hills. He described how he and his friends would "… just take ourselves off, sleep rough at weekends and holidays among moors and hills that were a very cheap bus ride away from the inner city where we lived… What we saw there was what we did not have in the close streets of the slums: trees, skies, clear rivers, space, unthreatened journeyings, a sense of an older landscape that had always been, from which we ourselves had come and to which we were now finding our ways back."

And yet in the distant days of the 1950s and 1960s, such "journeyings" were not always "unthreatened", because what Professor CEM Joad described as "the curse of the keeper" hung over those blue, fondly remembered hills. Since the Enclosure Acts of the eighteenth and nineteenth centuries, most of this once common land had been parcelled off to local landowners for their grouse shooting pleasure. Warning signs threatening trespassers sprang up at every access point, and burly stick- and gun-wielding gamekeepers patrolled the once-open moors. Only a dozen footpaths of two miles or more crossed the open moorland of the Peak District, and not one crossed the fifteen square miles of the ramblers' Holy Grail, the 2,000-foot summit of the Kinder Scout plateau.

*

Perrin was born in his grandparents' neat terraced house in Mabfield Road, Fallowfield, Manchester, in 1947. He lived there with his older sister until their parents "turned up" when he was six. His father's family were of Huguenot descent, had settled in North East Wales after their expulsion from France following the Revocation of the Edict of Nantes, and had followed the family trade of French polishing. Eventually the Perrin family moved to Salford and opened a furniture store at the bottom of Shudehill in Manchester. During the hungry 1930s, Perrin's father, Stanley, played rugby league for Salford: "He was the hooker, a hard little bugger. And he boxed." He began work as a housepainter and decorator (shades of Robert Tressell's *The Ragged Trousered Philanthropist*), and he married Perrin's mother, a nurse, in 1941.

When the Second World War broke out, Stanley enlisted in the Lancashire Fusiliers, was promoted to sergeant, and was posted to Orkney to command an anti-aircraft battery on Hoy – later the scene of one of Perrin's most memorable rock climbs on the vertiginous 450-foot-high sea stack of The Old Man of Hoy. It was with a perilous ascent of this – probably the most inaccessible summit in Britain – that Perrin chose to celebrate his sixtieth birthday in 2007.

His grandfather, who had fought in the Boer War, taught Perrin to read at the age of three from the few books in the house. They were John Bunyan's *The Pilgrim's Progress*, the Authorized Version of The Bible, the stately Jacobean prose rhythms of which often seem to chime with Perrin's, and *Pears' Cyclopaedia*. Together with an annual copy of *Old Moore's Almanack*, these four books constituted the entire library of his childhood.

Perrin speaks affectionately of his grandparents in his 1990 collection of essays, *Yes, to Dance*: "These two old people connected me back, through their stories and reminiscences the memory of which outcrops frequently into my more abstract adult consciousness, to the culture, values and beliefs of the pre-urban world of farm labour in Cheshire and on the Welsh Border in which they had grown up."

His returning parents eventually took their children away to live above a corner shop run by his father's sister in a dark, cobbled slum street in Hulme, across the Ship Canal from Salford's Pomona Docks: "I remember the smell of crumbling brick, the damp rosettes on the wall, the smallness of the room my sister and I shared," he wrote.

Perrin "unexpectedly" passed his 11-plus, went to a good grammar school where he lost his left eye in an accident – "it stopped me boxing, which disappointed my father" – and first took up walking and climbing. The weekly outdoor columns written by "Fellwalker" (Len Chadwick) in the *Oldham Evening Chronicle* had a huge influence on the young Perrin, who had met Chadwick by chance on a Ramblers' Association Sunday special excursion to Bala from Manchester's Victoria Station. He was to write a heartfelt obituary of him in the *Daily Telegraph*, something which would have amused the lifelong socialist Chadwick, when he died in 1988. Perrin described him as "the classic autodidact", and "a model of the columnist's craft".

In one of Perrin's earliest outings he recalls walking through Lyme Park and how he "…first panted up on the ridge running from Black Hill to Sponds Hill at the age of 12… by the track through the wood, where the clean brown loam lay bare beneath the trees, patched with vivid green moss and patterned by the brilliant orange of fallen beech leaves."

> After the wood's boundary wall, the path broached the steep moor to Bowstonegate. To arrive there was to encounter a vision which stopped my breath. Beyond were rocks, hills, valleys leading off among them, glimpses of a plain spreading westwards and still more hills on the farther side.

He carried on walking throughout that day and the next: scrambling on Windgather Rocks; racing across Cheshire's highest summit Shining Tor; climbing the "Cheshire Matterhorn" of Shutlingsloe; searching at Back Forest for the secret green cleft of Lud's Church; and finally following the

River Dane out towards the west, with the Welsh hills of his father's family in the faintest distance. "It is a journey which, in a sense, has never ended," he admits.

Perrin led his first rock climb – the Slab Climb on Wimberry Rocks in the Chew Valley above Greenfield – shortly before his thirteenth birthday. He describes it typically: "Its holds felt tiny, the risk immense, but in its course, I came into possession of my body. Rock-climbing then was a fearful risk, a self-preserving, cautious disrespect whose devotees owned no authority. That attitude inculcated, supported and developed in all spheres through the arguments of friends, you learn the steps of the dancing mind, which circles empty boasts but helps and coaxes on the novice honesty."

Perrin left school when he was seventeen after he had taken his A- Levels, just after his father's death from cancer. He moved to Wales and worked in the Gwydir Forest as a labourer, living in a tent. Then he joined the staff of the National Mountaineering Centre at Plas y Brenin as a climbing instructor and went on to the City of Oxford Outdoor Centre at Glasbury-on-Wye and to several other outdoor pursuit centres over the next few years.

By this time, and for over thirty years, Perrin was one of Britain leading rock climbers at the highest levels. In particular he helped to develop the potential for climbing the Pembrokeshire sea-cliffs – while constantly harassing the Ministry of Defence which restricted access to them because of the neighbouring NATO Castlemartin tank ranges.

Jim Perrin climbing on Stanage Slab, Peak District (Jim Perrin)

## WALKING CLASS HEROES

One of Perrin's most controversial climbs was of "Coronation Street" in Cheddar Gorge, Somerset. His "Street Illegal" essay account of that climb in the 1978 *Climbers' Club Journal* sparked huge controversy in the climbing world, because Perrin admitted he had done the climb after taking cocaine. His answer to the criticism was that at the time he was in a state of emotional crisis after his divorce from his first wife.

Later, "when I was getting creaky of joint and worn of limb," Perrin eventually went to university, turning down an offered place at Oxford to go to Bangor. He explains: "It was in Wales and nearer to the hills." Subsequently he was appointed Honorary Fellow at Bangor, and a Fellow of the Welsh Academy for services to Anglo-Welsh Literature.

His friendship with and admiration for Benny Rothman, leader of the 1932 Kinder Scout Mass Trespass (see Chapter 10) was a constant in his life. The company of the northern working-class people he had met in the outdoors at weekends had already shaped Perrin's political views and, he admits, was to have a major influence on his life. "Benny Rothman was a close friend. I belonged to the Young Communist League and later the Communist Party, and I have always campaigned not just for freedom of access to wild country but also against the monstrous crimes committed by the political right over the last forty years against the people of this country." Along with Rothman, Perrin spoke from platforms countrywide on issues like the Thatcher-led privatisation of water, while he campaigned for wider access to wild land and raised funds for the striking miners. He tells of how Rothman came up to him after one rabble-rousing performance, dug him in the ribs with his elbow, and cackled his approval: "You'll 'ave us flung in t'Tower, lad, if you carry on like that!" But Rothman's gleeful smile expressed approval for what his apprentice had said.

Perrin has been a keynote speaker at many annual Spirit of Kinder events, in celebration of Rothman and his brave band of trespassers from 1932. He told the seventieth anniversary event held at Bowden Bridge, Hayfield – starting point of the trespass – in 2002: "The more I got to know Benny, the more I appreciated the range and altruistic effort of his activity on behalf of the underprivileged and dispossessed in society. The connections with mountains and the environment were so slender a part of his life's work, however pivotal his actions on behalf of the outdoor community."

It was at that event that Andrew, the 11th Duke of Devonshire, famously and graciously apologised for the action of the landowners, including his own grandfather, in the 1930s. He completely stole the show, and I'll never forget the courteous action of Perrin when he got up and walked across the platform to shake the Duke's hand after his historic and dignified speech.

Perrin's own life has been dogged by tragedy. Nine months before the death from cancer of his partner Jacquetta, he lost his much-loved first-born son Will, a top climber himself, to suicide as he was about to embark on a Greenland expedition (he had suffered an accident on the Old Man of Hoy that affected his confidence). He recounts all this in his heart-rending, at times harrowing but never self-pitying book, *West* (2010).

Jim Perrin speaks at Spirit of Kinder rally (kindertrespass.org.uk)

Among the many awards and prizes Perrin has won are the coveted Boardman-Tasker Prize for Mountaineering Literature twice, in addition to frequent short-listings. His Boardman-Tasker prizes were for *Menlove* (1985), a biography of the 1930s gay climber John Menlove Edwards, and for *The Villain*, a biography of one of his working-class Mancunian rock climbing heroes, Don Whillans, in 2005. In addition, Perrin has won Mountaineering History and Mountain Literature Awards at the Banff Mountain Festival and the Kekoo Naoroji Award for Himalayan Literature. He has also been short-listed for the Wales Book of the Year and the Thomas Cook Travel Book of the Year.

Perrin has been an outspoken columnist and regular contributor to many national newspapers and outdoor and climbing magazines, including being a long-standing Country Diarist for the *Guardian*, and he has taught creative writing at the Writers' Centre for Wales and at Bath Spa and Leicester Universities.

Perhaps this eternal rebel's philosophy of life can be best summed up in a passage he wrote in *Travels with the Flea* (2002), a collection of his travel writings. (The Flea was his beloved Jack Russell terrier, a feisty and faithful partner in his wanderings for seventeen years):

> Measured against landscape, our intelligence goes awry. We look, we think, we assume, and yet these states are curiously insubstantial – histories, dates, achievements, yes, and we can catalogue, analyse, chronicle, record, log the data into our acquisitive minds and process it all but it is a blind. We desire nothingness… I call it nothingness, but really it is self-extinction, it is oneness, it is being a part.

# 16: How Marion Showed the Way
## Marion Shoard (1949-)

ENVIRONMENTAL CAMPAIGNER MARION SHOARD'S FIRST memories of the countryside are of the time when her father Harold used to take her out on their bikes to explore Minster Marshes on the Isle of Thanet, near her home in Ramsgate, east Kent. "The cattle-grazed pastures were criss-crossed by numerous drainage ditches which were brimming with life," she recalls. "I remember Dad drawing our net through the muddy water and drawing up masses of water weed, in which tiny creatures like newts, tadpoles, pond skaters and coiled water snails were climbing, wriggling and gliding. Those were wonderful days and I'll never forget them."

But in her twenties, she witnessed the loss through agricultural intensification of these much-loved places with their *de facto* public access, such as Minster Marshes, which were drained and converted into vast inaccessible arable fields. At that time, Shoard was living in the unlovely industrial town of Luton in Bedfordshire. She says, "At weekends I longed to ramble in the glorious, extensive woods and wide parkland which encircled a lovely lake at Luton Hoo, on the very edge of the town. But public access was almost completely barred. Travelling the length of breadth of Britain for my job and on holiday, I realised that the loss of informal rural playgrounds to modern farming on the one hand, and the barring of access from many of the most attractive landscapes that had escaped the plough on the other (often in the interests of game rearing or simply to preserve landowners' privacy), were widespread phenomena."

\*

Shoard was born in Redruth in west Cornwall in 1949 but she spent most of her childhood with her parents and brother John in Ramsgate, where she attended Clarendon House Grammar School for Girls. "I was inspired to enjoy the outdoors by my parents," she says. "My mother loved wildflowers and my father, who was then working as a radio telegraphist at the Meteorological Office, was a playful man who enjoyed taking risks. He used to take us climbing on the coastal cliffs at places like Pegwell Bay."

After leaving school she read zoology at St Hilda's College, Oxford, and developed an interest in animal behaviour. But during a short spell as an agricultural scientist at the University College of Wales in Cardiff she decided she needed to devote her energies to becoming a countryside conservationist. Initially she spent two years at the then Kingston-upon-Thames Polytechnic, studying for a diploma in town and country planning. Her dissertation examined the effectiveness of the Area of Outstanding Natural Beauty (AONB) designation, especially as it related to a part of the Chiltern Hills.

In 1973, Shoard joined the national office of the Council (now Campaign) for the Protection of Rural England (CPRE), as assistant secretary and its first full-time planning specialist. Shoard says she learned the value of a punchy press release from Chris Hall, the livewire former secretary of the Ramblers' Association, who was director of CPRE at the time, as well as from her former husband, the television journalist David Cox. For the next four years she lobbied in Parliament and campaigned in fields ranging from National Parks, forestry, and rural public transport to wildlife conservation.

It was during this time that Shoard became more and more convinced that the main threat to the beauty and diversity of England's countryside was the expansion and intensification of modern, industrial agriculture. With the help of a grant from the Sidney Perry Foundation, she left CPRE to go to the Centre of Environmental Studies to carry out research and write her first book, *The Theft of the Countryside*, which was published in 1980.

"This book seemed to strike a chord with the public and sparked off a lively debate, with no fewer than thirty letters published in *The Times*," she explains. "During the following few years I wrote articles and gave talks on the book's theme – frequently to groups of irate farmers and landowners – lobbied in Parliament during the passage of the Wildlife and Countryside Bill of 1980 and helped set up countryside action groups."

As well as urging the extension of planning control to take in major changes to the countryside wrought by farming and forestry and the re-creation of attractive landscapes (not unlike today's rewilding campaigns), *The Theft of the Countryside* put forward proposals to establish six new National Parks in lowland England. They were the Chilterns, Somerset Levels, Dorset Downs, Norfolk and Suffolk Broads, East Hampshire and West Sussex Downs, and the Lower Wye Valley and Vale of Herefordshire. The Broads and the South Downs, along with the New Forest, have since been designated as the first, predominantly lowland, National Parks.

Her second book *This Land is Our Land*, published in 1987, documented the 1,000-year struggle between landowners and the rest of the community for the control of the countryside, and put forward the idea of a new social contract between landowner and the landless. This book also attracted much media attention and as a result, Shoard presented a one-hour TV documentary on its subject for Channel 4 and called *Power in the Land*.

"One element of the social contract I had put forward was the replacement of the UK's trespass regime with a general right of public access to the countryside, providing much greater freedom to roam," she says.

With the help of grants from the Nuffield Foundation and The Leverhulme Trust, she set out to discover how such a right could operate on the ground, after making trips to Scandinavia, France and Germany to see for herself the very different access systems, such as the Scandinavian *Allemansrätten* ("everyman's right"), operating in those countries. Her conclusions on access were published in her award-winning book *A Right to Roam* (1999).

Shoard's trip in 1988 to Scandinavia for research on access for this book was the last time she took an aeroplane. In the field of eco-conscious transport, as in so many, she is something of a pioneer. She has never owned a car and almost all her research has been conducted either by bicycle, train or bus.

In *A Right to Roam* Shoard wrote: "The exclusion rights which landowners are trying to defend or sell are remnants of a feudal Britain whose day is gone. The obvious way to enable us all to use our countryside for recreation is to reclaim the birth right which was stolen from us with the Norman Conquest – the right to walk where we will. Access to the countryside is something which ought to be ours by right, like the vote or trial by jury... It would foster a new sense of oneness between people and their environment which none of the half-measures employed up till now could begin to achieve."

Three years after the publication of *A Right to Roam*, in an award-winning chapter in a book edited by Dame Jennifer Jenkins titled *Remaking the Landscape*, Shoard coined the term "edgelands" for the singular landscape that had been springing up in the late twentieth century in the urban fringe. Edgelands form that sometimes chaotic mix of rubbish tips and warehouses, superstores and derelict industrial plant, office parks, car scrapyards, allotments, fragmented farmland and unkempt wasteland frequently swathed in a riotous growth of wildflowers.

Shoard argued that the edgelands are both the powerhouse and the landscape of our own age. Yet, she claims, they go largely unplanned, seen by government and planners as a resource of brownfield land with little intrinsic value of their own. She explains:

> Edgelands can have great wildlife value, for instance. The variety of underlying rock and soil resulting from past human activity fosters biodiversity.
>
> What's more, the edgelands benefit from the absence of intensive farming and the resulting pollution of watercourses. And while our National Parks are often overgrazed by sheep, these unique but overlooked wildernesses find their own accommodation with Nature.

It was for her outstanding contribution towards the aim of promoting greater access to the countryside that Shoard was presented with the prestigious Golden Eagle award in 2010 by the Outdoor Writers' and Photographers' Guild. As Guild president, I was honoured to make the presentation to Shoard at the Guild's AGM in Anglesey. In her acceptance speech, she called on society to rid itself of the mental shackles which prevent people, particularly children, from taking full advantage of the spiritual and psychological benefits of the countryside. Presenting her with a David Bellamy painting, I said: "Marion, perhaps above all countryside writers, was responsible for creating the right political environment which allowed the passing of the Countryside and Rights of Way Act of 2000. And that, of course, eventually gave us the long-cherished but still unfinished and imperfect right to roam in open countryside."

*

For many years, Shoard has been fascinated by the way in which particular places have inspired poetry, painting and prose, such as the Helpston of John Clare (see Chapter 1) and the Laugharne of Dylan Thomas. She is a long-standing member of the Friends of the Dymock Poets, which celebrates the work of Edward Thomas, Rupert Brooke and Robert Frost, among others, and the landscape they loved on the borders of Worcestershire, Herefordshire and Gloucestershire. She explains: "When you're walking around that part of the country and imagining the people and landscapes the poets would have encountered, it's easy to see how it acted as a crucible for their creative ferment."

In the late 1990s, Shoard suddenly found herself propelled into another, entirely different, world. Her mother, then in her mid-eighties, developed dementia. "Suddenly, I was facing big decisions for which I was totally unprepared," she admits. "Should I look after my mother myself? Should she go and live in a care home and, if so, how could I choose one I could trust?" After a long struggle, she managed to secure good care for her mother in a long-term NHS

Marion Shoard (Liz Gregg)

facility. Typically, she then set about assembling the advice she wished had been available to her during what she says proved the most traumatic period of her life.

Just as her environment work uses innovative and exhaustive, independent research to examine whether and, if so, how the world should be changed, so too Shoard's work in the older people's field takes a radical new approach to what she found to be alarmingly uncharted territory. In *A Survival Guide to Later Life* (2004), she sought to provide straight-talking guidance for older people and their relatives. This was followed in 2017 by the encyclopaedic, 1,000-plus page, *How to Handle Later Life*.

One current area of concern for Shoard is the lack of

freedom to go outdoors faced by many of the thousands of older and disabled people living in care homes. Many of them rarely, if ever experience the joy of going into the open-air, even into the grounds of their homes. Shoard says: "Think what it would feel like to remain hermetically sealed day after day, communing only with man-made objects – the television and institutional plastics – and never feeling the kinship of the natural world. People in prison have a right to go outdoors for up to an hour a day; why shouldn't people in care homes enjoy something similar?"

Shoard now finds herself involved equally in older people's issues and environment affairs. She gives talks, writes articles and takes part in television and radio discussions, sometimes offering practical guidance, at other times polemical opinions and proposals to question current thinking. She is a vice-president of the British Association of Nature Conservationists, a volunteer with Healthwatch Medway and a committee member of Christians on Ageing. Circuitously and quite unintentionally, her involvement with an Alzheimer's Society group which evaluates research proposals has brought her back to the research aspects of her degree at Oxford half a century ago.

Shoard now lives on the banks of the River Medway in Strood, near Rochester, Kent. Her daughter Catherine, who seems to have inherited her mother's skill with words, is the film editor and a feature writer on *The Guardian*.

Jim Perrin, the distinguished outdoor writer (see Chapter 15), once described Shoard as "part of the great tradition of concerned and vigorous writers on the countryside who together comprise one of the uncelebrated glories of Britain's literature." Mild-mannered and never one to blow her own trumpet, Shoard has perhaps done as much as anybody to point out the injustices of land ownership in Britain, and to give us the freedom to roam in the countryside that we enjoy today. For that, we all owe her an enormous debt of gratitude.

# 17: Stravaiger John
## John Bainbridge (1953-)

**IT IS SIGNIFICANT THAT THE** email address of the redoubtable Dartmoor access campaigner and author John Bainbridge includes the word "stravaiger" – a Scottish term for a wanderer. Bainbridge describes himself as "an inveterate trespasser" and he is a passionate believer that access to the British countryside is the common heritage of all. "We should all be free to explore its mountains, hills, woods, rivers and coasts, with no superstitious reverence for legal property rights," he emphatically claims.

Born in the heart of the Black Country in West Bromwich, Bainbridge spent his early childhood exploring the countryside around Great Barr, Birmingham. "We lived on the West Bromwich side of Great Barr which then, even though it was close to the Black Country, was a great swathe of Green Belt countryside, bordered on one side by a long stretch of canal, and on the other sides by expanding housing and industry," he recalls. "But it was a farmed countryside, with animals in the fields and crops to be harvested, and we sometimes helped out on the farms.

"This was the first countryside I knew, and I had explored most of it on foot by the time I was five," says Bainbridge. "In those times, we would disappear all day into what seemed to us a wilderness, but which is sadly mostly gone now. I didn't know what a footpath was – I just wandered where I liked. And it's a habit I've always kept up in the years since."

As he grew older, Bainbridge would often be out roaming all day along the canal, sometimes getting lifts back on the then still-working narrow boats. His parents were not great walkers, but every Sunday he was taken for long walks by "Uncle Charlie" – not a real uncle but a dustman who had been a neighbour of his grandparents. "Me and Uncle Charlie walked miles, exploring old coal mines, visiting gypsy camps, and exploring some very interesting corners of the Black Country," he recollects. "Sometimes, we'd go out to the sandstone outcrop of Kinver Edge, where I learned to scramble on rock, or up to the gritstone moors of the Roaches in the Staffordshire Moorlands."

When he went to Hamstead Primary School, next to a working coal mine, he never liked it very much. "It got in the way of my roaming," he explains. "The headmaster used to threaten us that if we didn't work hard at school we'd end up working even harder down the mine."

Bainbridge did not even take the 11-plus but went to the newly-built Dartmouth Comprehensive School, which was a three-mile walk across countryside and by the canal. "Sometimes," confesses "Stravaiger" John, "I'd get so entranced by the walk I'd bunk off school and just keep on walking."

At the time, the Bainbridge family spent most of their holidays with relatives at Teignmouth in south Devon. The young Bainbridge would walk the coast path and in the Haldon Hills above the town, and it was from there he first got to know Dartmoor. When he was thirteen, the family moved house to Teignmouth, and Bainbridge went to the West Lawn School in the town.

It was from Teignmouth that he began to explore Dartmoor on foot, often on long camping trips, some of which could last for months at a time. He became passionate and very knowledgeable about the tors and moors of his beloved Dartmoor, which is sometimes still called "the last wilderness in Southern Britain".

"When I left school, my first real job was as a postman in Teignmouth," he says. "We did long hours in those days, with split shifts and compulsory overtime. I began to understand the concept of being 'a free man on Sunday' (as Ewan MacColl put it in his famous ramblers' anthem *The Manchester Rambler*), although it was usually only three Sundays out of four, because we all had to take a turn at Sunday collections."

So even with a full-time job at that time, Bainbridge was constantly out walking. He sometimes took very long tramps across England, where he would frequently sleep rough, keeping up his habit of walking wherever he liked, across the great estates and other forbidden lands. On one occasion, as he relates in his 2013 book, *The Compleat Trespasser: Journeys into the Heart of Forbidden Britain*, an irate gamekeeper on a large Devon estate peppered him and his friend Jack with his shotgun. "I resisted Jack's suggestion that we head for a hospital or the constabulary," he wrote. "Both options seemed unsporting. Trespassing was a game we played, and we had to abide both by its rules and consequences."

Bainbridge spent most of the mid-1980s working voluntarily as press officer for the Dartmoor Badger Protection League, at one time spending months on end living wild in a Dartmoor wood in a bid to save its badgers from the threatened government cull.

In 1989, with just one Open University Credit (he had no A-Levels) Bainbridge became a mature student at the University of East Anglia, where he read for a major in literature and a minor in nineteenth-century social history. "They were three happy years," he recalls, "which also gave me the opportunity to explore – and to trespass – in East Anglia."

It was not long after moving to Teignmouth that he had first joined the Ramblers Association and the Dartmoor Preservation Association (DPA). He became a walks leader for the RA and was soon on its area council, later becoming the Devon Area Footpaths Secretary and representing the RA at footpath inquiries. Bainbridge recalls: "I first met Sylvia Sayer (see Chapter 9) at that time and was greatly influenced by her. I joined the DPA Executive Committee, on which I served for several years. At the time, Dartmoor was under massive threat from clay-mining, military training and reservoirs."

After serving on the executive, Bainbridge became the chief executive of the DPA between 1996 and 2005 and achieved a number of successes in protecting the ever-threatened Dartmoor National Park. These included leading the victorious campaign to save the archaeologically important Shaugh Moor and the Blackabrook Valley from waste tipping and quarrying by the china clay industry. He also led the campaign for the

John Bainbridge on the Howgill Fells (John Bainbridge)

right to roam in Devon, which culminated in the Countryside and Rights of Way Act of 2000. "It was also an interesting time for access battles," he adds. "The new Blair Labour government was getting the CRoW Act through, but some landowners were trying to keep walkers out of parts of Dartmoor. This was sad, because there had long been a tradition of *de facto* access on the Moor."

An example of this conflict was the fight to restore access to the Hensroost Mine Track, an ancient path near Hexworthy which was closed by the landowner, the Prince of Wales and his tenants, despite having been free for ramblers to use for centuries.

Bainbridge says: "I made a point of trespassing along it on a monthly basis and gave evidence at unsuccessful public inquiries. Access was finally restored under the CRoW Act, and the Ramblers gave me the great honour of leading the first legal walk." He also fought hard to restore access to the closed-off Vixen Tor, again trespassing frequently in that still unresolved battle. He explains: "I campaigned for CRoW because I thought it was the least worst option. But I've always thought we needed complete access to the land, such as the Scots and the Scandinavians enjoy. And I'd like to see organisations like the Ramblers recover some of their original militancy."

While he was with the DPA, Bainbridge also consistently opposed the continuing military presence on Dartmoor, for which he was praised by Anthony Steen MP in the House of Commons in 2003. He served for nine years as a representative on the Council (now Campaign) for National Parks, and in 2012 he was commended for his campaigning work by the Ramblers to mark his forty-year contribution to the outdoors movement.

He left the DPA in 2005 because he felt it was becoming too close to the Dartmoor establishment. "When Sylvia Sayer gave up the DPA, she said she was going 'to be a freelance, with the emphasis on the lance!' I decided that would be my motto too." By this time he had become a full-time writer and a freelance Dartmoor guide, but when these activities got in the way of his own ramblings, he stopped them, except for leading the occasional ramblers' walks. He says: "I decided I would begin to write about the countryside and walking, though I never made much money from it and, at the time of Margaret Thatcher, spent long periods on the dole, volunteering as a kind of political bandit and flying picket. They were rough and sometimes violent times, but they did give me the opportunity to extend my trespass territories."

In 2009 Bainbridge created the Teignmouth and Dawlish Way long-distance footpath, writing the guidebook of the same name, and with the late Joe Turner he also helped establish the route of the Two Moors Way long-distance trail, a 103-mile coast-to-coast route which links the Dartmoor and Exmoor National Parks, which opened in 1976. He was also a founder committee member of the Two Moors Way Association.

He moved to Cumbria in 2011 because he says he wanted to walk the Lakeland fells and to be nearer to the Scottish mountains "while I was still young enough to enjoy them." "I also wanted somewhere peaceful to write my books and I

was finding it increasingly hard to escape the Dartmoor label."
Bainbridge married his long-time partner and friend Annie at
Gretna Green in December in 2019.

Still an unapologetic trespasser, Bainbridge remains a
steadfast campaigner for countryside access. He dealt with the
subject of trespassing in his controversial book *The Compleat
Trespasser*, which explores why the British were – and in many
instances still are – denied responsible access to much of their
land. He briefly touched on the same subject in his book on
walking – *Rambling - the Beginner's Bible*. He has also written
an e-book about one of his own heroes, the Victorian writer and
walker George Borrow, and he is also the author of a walking
autobiography entitled *Wayfarer's Dole*. He has even found time
to publish half a dozen thriller novels, and one of his heroes in
a couple of them is a veteran of the 1932 Kinder Scout Mass
Trespass. He admits that he often inserts bits of trespassing
autobiography into his books. As an outdoor journalist,
Bainbridge has contributed to most outdoor magazines and
he is the author of over thirty books about British topography,
including the Dorset Coast, South Devon Coast and Newton
Abbot, Torbay, the Cotswolds and Worcestershire.

How does he sum up his philosophy of access to the
countryside and trespassing in particular? "There is a long
and historic tradition of trespassing in Britain. It is a hugely
important part of our social history," as he emphasises in *The
Compleat Trespasser*.

Why shouldn't the British people have free access to the
best bits of our own countryside? Many of our parents
and grandparents fought for this country in the World
Wars. Some of my readers may well have served in more
recent conflicts. Why is it deemed okay to be prepared
to die for your country, but not be allowed to walk
across it?

# 18: Campaigning Kate
## Kate Ashbrook (1955-)

THE BRIGHT SPRING MORNING OF Thursday 20 April 1972 was a day that was to change the life of Kate Ashbrook, campaigning general secretary of Britain's oldest national conservation body, the Open Spaces Society. That was the day she first met her mentor, lifelong friend and redoubtable Dartmoor champion Lady Sylvia Sayer (see Chapter 9). It was a close friendship which was to last for nearly three decades, and one which influenced Ashbrook into becoming one of the most effective and outspoken campaigners for access rights in Britain today.

The meeting took place at Sayer's ancient, thatched granite Dartmoor longhouse home of Old Middle Cator, near Widecombe-in-the Moor. She had first seen Sayer in action the previous year, at a public meeting called about the proposed Swincombe Reservoir on southern Dartmoor. "I sat at the back of the crowded hall, feeling increasingly angry as speaker after speaker condemned lovely Swincombe as a useless bog," recalls Ashbrook. "Then, to the shame of the assembled company, Syl stood up and spoke with courage and eloquence about the value of wild country for our wellbeing. I knew then I must campaign for it. I also knew that I must meet her."

Ashbrook continues: "I can still picture that first meeting, in the small, dark sitting-room, with Syl and her husband Guy, their son Oliver his wife Janet and three granddaughters. I can recall the Cator smell: the welcoming hearth in the centre of the cottage generated warmth and the aroma of damp wood and peat."

At the tender age of seventeen, Ashbrook had already joined the Dartmoor Preservation Association, of which Sayer was chairman, a post she had held since 1951. She retired from the chair in 1973 to become a patron.

Ashbrook adds: "It was Syl who taught me how to be a

campaigner. I emulated her style and learnt that it is vital to be tough and fearless, never to start by compromising or you give away too much, and never to give up."

And it was Sayer who gave Kate her initial introduction to the national conservation and access scene. She invited her to take her place on the committee of the Commons, Open Spaces and Footpaths Preservation Society (later to become the Open Spaces Society) in 1978, and the Council (later Campaign) for National Parks in 1983. She also persuaded her to go to the Ramblers Association's general council as a Devon Area delegate in 1982, which enabled her to be elected to the executive committee that year.

The other person from whom Ashbrook says she might have inherited her campaigning zeal was her aunt, Nancy Balfour, an *Economist* journalist and editor and art collector. Last year, Ashbrook was delighted to be able to donate Balfour's Barbara Hepworth bronze sculpture *Orpheus* (*Maquette 1*) to the Hepworth Gallery in Wakefield.

Ashbrook was born in 1955 and brought up at Wrango, a gracious Queen Anne house in the centre of Denham, an unspoilt village deep in the south Buckinghamshire green belt. Her father, John (known as Jay) was an American born in Wisconsin who met his wife Margaret Balfour when she was in the Land Army during the Second World War. They married in 1948. Her father sold food to US bases in England, later moving into publishing.

Kate Ashbrook, their first born, was educated at Benenden School, Cranbrook, Kent and Exeter University, where she gained a Bachelor of Science honours degree in biology. She later did part-time work for Anthony Steen, MP for South Hams, who was sponsoring Devon County Council's Dartmoor Commons Bill. The bill, which passed into law in 1985, provided public access on foot and horseback to much of Britain's great southern wilderness of Dartmoor.

Ashbrook was a committee member of the Dartmoor Preservation Association for ten years between 1974 and 1984, and honorary secretary between 1981 and 1984. She became president between 1995 and 2011 and has been a trustee since 2011.

While she was with the DPA, she helped persuade the china clay companies to give up their fifty-year-old consents for damaging quarrying and waste dumping on Dartmoor, without claiming any compensation. Ashbrook joined the Open Spaces Society as general secretary in 1984.

In 1978, the Department for Transport announced that it wanted to drive the dual-carriageway Okehampton bypass south of the town through the Dartmoor National Park. This was hugely controversial and contravened not only National Park policies but also the Department of Environment's own advice circular on new roads in National Parks. This stated that "no new route for long-distance traffic should be constructed through a national park... unless it has been demonstrated that there is a compelling need which would not be met by any reasonable alternative means."

"Of course, there were other reasonable alternatives," says Ashbrook, who represented the Open Spaces Society at the record nine-month-long public inquiry. "It was not a foregone conclusion that any bypass was needed but, if one was, it should have gone to the north, across low-grade farmland not through the priceless medieval deer park of Okehampton Castle." But the case was lost and the bypass built, creating a dangerous precedent for the future in other National Parks.

\*

Perhaps the action Ashbrook will be best remembered for was when, acting in a personal capacity, in 2002 she won an Appeal Court ruling (R (Ashbrook) v East Sussex County Council) condemning East Sussex County Council for its failure to remove illegal obstructions from Framfield Footpath 9 – the infamous "Hoogstraten" footpath. In February, 2003, Ashbrook was invited to wield the bolt cutters to free the footpath after thirteen years of illegal obstruction. It had been blocked by Rarebargain, a company associated with the millionaire property tycoon Nicholas van Hoogstraten, who had publicly condemned all ramblers as "riff raff" and "scum of the earth".

A proud Ashbrook recalls: "Surrounded by film crews, photographers, broadcasters and journalists, we witnessed and celebrated the demolition of the barn which had blocked the path, padlocked gates, container-sized refrigeration units and barbed-wire fence which had ostentatiously prevented the public from enjoying the ancient path for so many years."

It was the culmination of a long campaign and a victory over a landowner who had intimidated walkers, the highway authority and the police; and over a highway authority which had failed in its duty to "assert and protect the right of the public to the use and enjoyment of the highway."

Because of the difficulties and unpleasantness associated with the path, the county council had left it in an obstructed condition for years and then – caving in to the landowner – set up a diversion order around the obstructions instead of removing them. Prosecutions of Rarebargain, first by the Ramblers and then by Ashbrook herself, resulted in orders against the company to remove the obstructions, and fines and costs totalling £93,250 – which have never been paid.

Ashbrook took the county council to court for diverting instead of clearing the path, and won in the appeal court with a judgment which reprimanded the council for ignoring the fact that the obstructions were wilful and that the magistrates had ordered their removal, and for flouting its own policy on the diversion of blocked paths.

Rarebargain later went into liquidation, but the liquidator agreed to unblock the path and when it was reopened, allowed Ashbrook and the Ramblers on the site to win maximum publicity for their cause. Ashbrook commented: "The high profile reopening of the 'Hoogstraten path', backed by a court of appeal judgment that highway authorities must carry out their statutory duties to remove obstructions instead of seeking diversions around them, certainly helped our cause." "But all is not yet sweetness and light," she adds. "Hoogstraten and his successors were blatant lawbreakers, but others are more insidious. Whether they plough up and plant crops on public paths, or erect intimidating gates and CCTV cameras, they are effectively deterring lawful users. There are still plenty of mini-Hoogstratens around… Where persuasion fails, we must be ready to use the courts and publicity to free our paths, as we did at Framfield."

Ashbrook became the first woman and youngest-ever chair of the Ramblers' Association between 1995-8, between 2006 and 2009 and currently between 2018 and 2021. She was vice-chair between 1993 and 1995 and between 2017 and 2018 and has been a committee member or trustee since 1982. She was chair of the Ramblers' access committee from its inception in 1997 and, since 1991, of the access working party and access panel which had preceded it. These committees were concerned with drafting and promoting the 2000 Countryside and Rights of Way (CRoW) Act freedom to roam legislation.

Acting on behalf of the Ramblers, Ashbrook was particularly active in seeing the CRoW Bill through Parliament, as she followed all the debates in both Houses and in committee, promoting amendments and providing briefings.

Ashbrook was chair of the Campaign for National Parks between 2003 and 2009, vice-chair between 1998 and 2003 and 2016 and 2019, and committee member or trustee between 1983 and 2019. She was also a board member of the Countryside Agency from its inception in 1999 until its sad demise in 2006.

Ashbrook has been a regular speaker at the annual Spirit of Kinder events, which are held in celebration of the 1932 Mass Trespass. At the 2014 event held at Sheffield Town Hall, she eloquently expressed her feelings about the need to continue the right-to-roam campaign post-CRoW. "The CRoW Act of 2000 was an important milestone, but we still have much to achieve," she said. "And it's become harder than ever. We have a government which is obsessed with development, money comes before everything and green spaces everywhere are at risk. There is plenty of evidence that walking and outdoor recreation are good for the economy and for our health and wellbeing. The

Kate Ashbrook celebrates the passing of the CRoW Act (Kate Ashbrook)

growth in Walkers Are Welcome Towns demonstrates that local businesses know that it helps to welcome walkers.

"The evidence on health is overwhelming – it makes sense to transfer money from the Health Service into paths and access provision. Yet our paths are in crisis. Councils are now so desperate they seem not to care that they have a legal duty to maintain public paths." She added: "There is plenty we can do to ensure that our rights are not undermined. We must show that open spaces, paths, access and freedom are vital human needs not luxuries. "We are not a fringe group, we are mainstream," she concluded. "We change lives and we save lives."

*

In the current edition of *Who's Who*, Kate Ashbrook lists her recreations as "pedantry, finding illegally blocked footpaths, and learning British birdsong". Following that last hobby, she surveyed for the British Trust for Ornithology's bird atlas between 2007 and 2011 and since 2007 has carried out the Breeding Bird and other surveys.

Her love of birds and birdsong is perhaps best expressed in a blog that Ashbrook wrote after her annual April early morning walk up Tavy Cleave on western Dartmoor in 2019, in search of the mountain blackbird or ring ouzel. The walk had a particular significance for Ashbrook because it passes the waterfall where Sylvia Sayer's father, Richard Munday, had proposed marriage to her mother, Olive Burnard, in 1891. "I followed the path alongside the leat and soon after I rounded the bend into the cleave I could hear one calling, with its clear toots (three, sometimes four). It flew across from the south and sat on a mossy rock," she wrote, noting that the RSPB had reported two pairs nesting in the cleave that year.

That year Ashbrook reported that she had seen 116 different species of birds – four more than the year before – and heard three more – Cetti's, grasshopper and wood warblers – in her wanderings around England and Wales.

Campaigner Kate – as she is known on her blog – still manages to keep an eagle eye on any threats to our rights to access the countryside, and long may she continue to do so. In her 2014 Spirit of Kinder speech, Ashbrook recalled the spirit of the 1932 trespassers through the words of Nelson Mandela: "Vision without action is only dreaming. Action without vision is only passing time. But vision with action can change the world."

# 19: Grande Dame of Conservation
## Fiona Reynolds (1958-)

CNICHT (FROM THE OLD ENGLISH variant of "knight") is a shapely Snowdonia peak rising sharply above the pastures of Croesor and the Glaslyn valley like a miniature Matterhorn. It is only when you reach its 2,265-foot summit that you realise it is actually the southern terminus of a rocky ridge, but the views from top surely make up for the knight's innocent deception.

It is also where Fiona Reynolds, Grande Dame of British landscape conservation, experienced what she describes as her "heartfelt epiphany" when, at the age of seven, she climbed her first mountain. She vividly recalls the moment in her 2016 book, *The Fight for Beauty*:

> My father took my older sister and me, soon after dawn, to climb Cnicht, a miraculous little Matterhorn-shaped mountain nestled in the hills of Snowdonia behind Porthmadog.
>
> It was the mid-1960s and we proudly laced our school shoes and stowed our Pac-a-Macs, specially purchased for holiday walking. Cnicht… rises steeply, its summit hidden behind a series of ridges and mini summits as you ascend. We took most of the morning to scale it, the excitement of breaching each horizon dashed as another loomed before us. But the moment when we reached the top has never left me.
>
> The peaks and ridges of Snowdon and the Glyderau to the north; the bulk of Cadair Idris to the south; the Moelwyns to the east, littered with the poignant remains of mining communities; and the azure blue sweep of Cardigan Bay to the west, with Harlech's sandy beach and our tiny holiday cottage… in the foreground.

Cnicht, Snowdonia (Velela/Wikimedia Commons)

Reynolds reflected: "I had never before seen such beauty, never before felt the shiver of nature's exquisite perfection, never before experienced the sense of striving then reaching a summit, from which we could survey, it felt, the whole glorious world."

Unbeknown to the girl who was to become the future director general of the National Trust, Cnicht would later benefit from one of the Trust's most successful forays into what would now be called "crowd-funding" appeals, when the Hafod y Llan estate was put up for sale in the summer of 1986 with an asking price of £3.6 million. Kicked off by a £1 million donation by Oscar-winning Hollywood star and proud Welshman Sir Anthony Hopkins and boosted by further generous contributions by the Welsh rock group the Stereophonics and the general public, the appeal swiftly raised £5 million, and the Trust successfully acquired the estate.

That Cnicht revelation and many other explorations and experiences in the countryside gave Reynolds an idyllically happy childhood, as she was brought up as the second of five sisters by her countryside-loving father and mother in the then concrete-producing town of Rugby, Warwickshire. Although born in what is claimed to be the highest town in England at Alston in Cumbria, Reynolds spent most of her childhood in Warwickshire, where she and her sisters all attended Rugby High School for Girls. "My parents – my father was a metallurgist and my mother a geography teacher – were both passionate countryside lovers, and all our holidays involved walking, climbing and exploring," she explains.

Winning a place at the all-women Newnham College, Cambridge, in 1976, Reynolds won a first-class honours degree in geography and land economy, followed by an MPhil degree in land economy. Her introduction to the world of countryside conservation and campaigning came with her appointment as secretary of the Council for National Parks in 1980. The Council (now Campaign) for National Parks was formed from the Standing Committee on National Parks eighty years ago, and included representatives from the Ramblers' Association, Youth Hostels Association and the Councils for the Protection of Rural England (CPRE) and Wales (CPRW). It was then based in tiny, cramped offices in London's Hobart Place.

I first met Reynolds when I was Head of Information Services for the Peak District National Park, and we enjoyed many exciting years of campaigning together during the National Parks Awareness Campaign between 1984 and 1987. Her challenging and inspiring speech at the outdoor rally which I organised at Cave Dale, just outside Castleton, in June 1986 was a highlight of the event. "Let's ask ourselves a question," she told the assembled audience of about 1,000 people. "Who cares about National Parks? Of course we do, we all care, otherwise we wouldn't be here in this beautiful location on this lovely afternoon. But do we care enough, do we really care about National Parks?"

She pointed out that a recent survey had shown that a tiny percentage of the population knew anything about National Parks, and only about half could name more than one, and that was thirty-five years after the parks had been designated. "It's not good enough," Reynolds insisted. "If we all cared about National Parks, would that be enough? No, it wouldn't. National Parks are not only a national treasure and a national glory – they are a national responsibility." And she called on the government and all its agencies to show by their actions that they equally cared about the National Parks.

Working with presidents such as Everest mountaineer Lord John Hunt and broadcaster Brian Redhead, Reynolds converted the CNP from the cosy but largely defunct (now that the Parks were in place) body of the Standing Committee into a lively, campaigning organisation which grabbed the headlines and put the plight of the underfunded Parks firmly into the public eye.

Reynolds left CNP in 1987 to join the Council (now Campaign) for Rural England (CPRE) first as assistant director (policy), then becoming director of the organisation in 1992. Under her leadership, the charity, which aims to protect the English countryside from harmful development, grew both in in size and influence. She was awarded the CBE in 1998 for services to the countryside and environment, before being tempted away from her role in countryside conservation in 1998 to head up the newly created Women's Unit in Tony Blair's Labour government's Cabinet Office. While there she says she took a research and evidence-based approach to show how embracing diversity would benefit both society and the economy, at the same time gaining significant and valuable experience of working within the Civil Service at a senior level.

But the call of the countryside was strong, and in January 2001 Reynolds took up a new and even more challenging role as director general of Britain's biggest countryside charity, the five-million-member National Trust. She led a programme of change, updating the organisation's structures and management. The significant changes made under Reynolds' leadership included staff restructuring and the relocation of the Trust's national headquarters from London to a new "green" office in Swindon, a major strategic financial review and a major overhaul of the organisation's governance.

In the twelve years under Reynolds' leadership, Trust membership grew from 2.7 million in 2001 to four million by the time she left. The number of paying visitors to Trust properties rose from ten million to nineteen million, its turnover more than doubled from £200 million to around £450 million, and its commercial profit trebled to £24 million per annum.

The range and diversity of properties owned by the Trust also widened in Reynolds' time, including places like the Birmingham back-to-back terraces and the lavishly-decorated Georgian terraced home of the Kenyan-born poet, Khadambi Asalache in Wandsworth Road, Lambeth, in central London. A significant number of coast and countryside properties, all of which honour the Trust's longstanding policy of open access and inalienability, were also acquired. To wide acclaim, Reynolds also led the Trust's contribution to restoring balance to the land use planning system, and she was centrally involved in ensuring a secure future for England's public forests.

Above all in Reynolds' time at the Trust, she ensured that the once occasionally stuffy and buttoned-up conservative organisation became warmer and more welcoming in its approach. Typical of this was the idea of the list of fifty things children should do before they were 11¾. These included climbing and rolling down a huge hill; camping outdoors and cooking on a campfire; clambering over rocks and taking a friend on a nature ramble. She explains: "Using accessible subjects such as local food, a passion for history, nature and the outdoors, children's play, gardening and energy saving, we showed how looking after beautiful places for ever and for everyone could demonstrate the benefits of valuing things beyond the material."

Reynolds was made a Dame of the British Empire (DBE) in 2008 in recognition of her work with the National Trust and for services to heritage.

In 2013, Reynolds returned to academia and became the first-ever female Master of Emmanuel College, Cambridge, which was established in the sixteenth century, and this remains her current position. In an article in the *Guardian* she described it as her "third glass ceiling" after her challenging spells at CPRE and the National Trust. Typically, at Emmanuel she is launching an "open arms" project which aims to improve the college's educational and community facilities, and to enhance support for the post-doctorate community in the city of Cambridge.

Reynolds also joined the board of Wessex Water in 2012, where she leads on sustainability issues and chairs the company's Futures Panel, which

Grande Dame of Conservation: Fiona Reynolds (Fiona Reynolds)

helps to shape its future long-term strategies. In 2018, she was appointed a trustee of the Grosvenor Estate, one of the largest privately-owned international property companies developing, managing and investing in property in more than sixty cities, and owned by the billionaire Duke of Westminster. Reynolds explains this appointment thus: "I am particularly interested in sustainable development of the urban and rural landscape, and how a family trust can ensure that its long-term interest in land and property contributes to wider societal and environmental needs."

Reynolds married Bob Merrill in 1981, and the family home is in the heart of the Gloucestershire Cotswolds, although much of Reynolds' time is now spent in Cambridge. The couple have three grown-up daughters. She lists her personal interests as "obsessively" walking, landscape history, historical buildings and classical music and opera. "Music played a huge part in my childhood," she explains. "I played the viola in a number of local orchestras when I lived in Warwickshire."

\*

As a keen walker, access to the countryside has always been one of Reynolds' key passions. She has attended and spoken at many of the annual Spirit of Kinder celebrations of the 1932 Mass Trespass. In *The Fight for Beauty* she movingly describes the genesis of the access movement:

> Since the early 19th century the working population had sought to escape their poor living and working conditions in the cities by finding joy and freedom on foot or bicycle outside them. This was particularly the case in the northern cities where the fells rose enticingly from almost the city boundaries. But the limits to people's enjoyment were brutally clear, since the hills were effectively closed to them.
>
> Since the middle of the 19th century there had been repeated, failed, attempts to legalise free access to mountains and open country, and rising frustration that landowners were able to exclude people from places – often former common lands which were felt to "belong to no man".

It would not be until the passing of the Countryside and Rights of Way Act in 2000 that free open access to mountain and moorland was obtained, offering, said Reynolds, "the experience of beauty and freedom the factory workers had sought".

Perhaps the best summing up of Reynolds' character was in author Adam Nicolson's review of her "deeply inspiring" *The Fight for Beauty*. He wrote: "It is a fascinating story told by someone who has lived and worked at the heart of the struggle for more than 30 years: clear, analytical, principled and impassioned but never dodging the economic and political realities."

That's a fair description of the "Grande Dame" of the conservation of Britain's precious countryside.

# 20: Conclusion
## The Right to Roam

A COUPLE OF YEARS AGO with my good Swedish friend Maria I enjoyed a pleasant stroll through the ancient ash, elm and oak woodlands of the Borgen Nature Reserve in the Råån valley near Helsingborg, in the Skåne district of southern Sweden. The reserve takes its "burgh" name from the still-visible earthworks of the original Iron Age hillfort, now occupied by the redbrick ruins of Vallåkra castle on a hill above the Råån. Vallåkra is probably most famous today for its hand-thrown stoneware pottery. On the site of several former coal mines, the pottery still relies on the 180-million-year-old Jurassic clay to provide the raw material for the pots, and the coal still provides fuel for the ovens. In 1970, the clays also famously revealed the footprints of the twenty-foot-long herbivorous dinosaur Plateosaurus.

With my wife Val happily ensconced in the picturesque pottery, Maria and I started our walk. As we strolled by the rushing waters of the Fjärestadsbäcken and Härslövsån streams on a broad track through the mossy forest, I marvelled at the rich flora of the understorey. Mosses and liverworts – sure signs of a pure and clean atmosphere – hung from every branch of the leafless trees and decorated the rocks in the streams, and the mysterious fruiting bodies of fungi sprouted luxuriantly from the forest floor. I half expected to see a troll emerge at every turn. Apparently – and although common in Britain, a real rarity in Sweden and in the rest of the Continent – misty drifts of bluebells carpet the woodland floor in springtime.

We eventually came to an inviting-looking hill above a bridged river crossing, and Maria volunteered: "Come on. Let's see what's at the top." So off we set, knowing full well that under the enlightened Swedish right of *Allemansrätten*, literally no man could stop us. I reflected that if that same urge had taken us in an English forest, we could have been accused of trespass and eviction by an irate landowner with the traditional cartoon greeting of "Get orf my land!"

Earlier we had enjoyed the same sense of freedom given by *Allemansrätten* while exploring the magnificent coastal cliff-top situation of the Ales Stenar Bronze Age ship-shaped standing stones. We'd walked up from the tiny fishing village of Kåseberga just as a blood red sun — we later learned it was caused by a Saharan dust cloud — rose over the Baltic Sea, casting a strange, ethereal light over the fifty-nine enigmatic stones.

# ALLEMANSRÄTTEN –SÅ FUNKAR DEN!

Jag håller mig tillräckligt långt bort från någons hem.

Jag tältar bara så länge jag får och där jag får.

Jag eldar inte på klippor eller om det finns en brandrisk.

Jag tar med mig mitt skräp.

Jag vet hur jag gör mina behov i skogen.

Jag skadar inte skog och mark.

Jag stänger alltid grinden.

Jag plockar bara de blommor, svampar och bär som jag får plocka.

Jag håller koll på vad som gäller när jag är i ett skyddat område.

Jag har koll på min hund.

Jag visar alltid hänsyn mot djur och människor i naturen.

Jag badar där jag får och jag lägger min båt där det är okej.

Jag kör bara motorfordon där jag får.

HÅLL SVERIGE RENT®

153

Enshrined in the constitution of Sweden's General Court, the universal right of *Allemansrätten* ("everyman's right"), is not actually a law, and neither is there a law which precisely defines it. But the right is protected by laws that set common-sense limits on what is permissible and what is not. The right of public access can be interpreted in court, but I understand that in practice, cases relating to it are few and far between.

In Sweden, this universal right of access is quite rightly regarded as part of the country's cultural heritage, at times even as a national symbol. The concept of "universal right" is probably no older than the last century, but its principle can be traced far back in the country's history. The Swedish government's booklet on the subject puts it simply: "The right of public access is a fantastic opportunity for all of us to roam freely in nature. You can make use of the right of public access when you go for a walk in the forest, paddle a kayak, go climbing or just sit on a rock and think. Usually it is completely natural for us. In order for everyone to enjoy nature, we need to take care of nature and wildlife and show consideration for landowners and others who are outdoors."

The guiding and qualifying principle is summed up in four words: "Don't disturb – don't destroy."

\*

Many people, including most of those featured in this book, believe that England and Wales should adopt this proven Swedish model, which gives walkers the right to roam anywhere subject to a common-sense set of restrictions. Either that or the Scottish version under its enlightened Land Reform Act of 2003, which gave legal backing to the traditional *de facto* unrestricted rights of public access to the countryside.

The situation in Scotland, where access to open country had historically been allowed subject to deer stalking restrictions, has always been slightly different. Following intense lobbying by Ramblers Scotland, led by former director Dave Morris and people like Rennie McOwan (see Chapter 11) the Land Reform Act was introduced and established a statutory right to be on land for recreational, educational and certain other purposes and also the right to cross land. These rights have to be exercised responsibly as specified in the Scottish Outdoor Access Code, which celebrates its fifteenth anniversary in 2020. In a year which also marks the twenty-fifth anniversary of Ramblers Scotland, there is also to be a review of open access in Scotland.

Yet given the almost feudal intransigence of many English landowners, and the inordinate length of time (well over a century) it took to regain public access to mountain and moorland, is this just a fanciful pipe dream for optimistic access campaigners and something which can never be achieved?

The thorny question of "who owns Britain?" goes back centuries, and many of today's problems over access to the countryside can be traced back to the invasion of William the Conqueror on the date every schoolchild remembers – 1066. Nineteen years after his successful invasion, William commissioned the comprehensive Domesday survey of his newly-acquired kingdom, which precisely described exactly who owned what and where so he could extract maximum tax returns from them. It also records how many former Saxon estates had been granted to the new Norman overlords who had been supporters of William in his successful invasion. Nine centuries later, when asked what advice he would give to young entrepreneurs wanting to succeed in modern Britain, one of Britain's wealthiest men, the late 6th Duke of Westminster, replied: "Make sure you have an ancestor who was a very close friend of William the Conqueror."

The apparent injustice of the system of land ownership in Britain was criticised by the unlikeliest of proponents in the future Tory Prime Minister, Winston Churchill, who wrote in *The People's Rights* published in 1909: "Land ... is by far the greatest of monopolies." He asked his readers to consider the wealth which came to the landlord who happened to own a plot of land on the outskirts or at the centre of one of our great cities. He only needed to wait, claimed Churchill, while others worked and paid taxes to make the city grow more prosperous, build businesses, install roads and railways, and pay for schools, hospitals and other public amenities. "All the while," fumed Churchill, "the land monopolist has only to sit still and watch complacently his property multiplying in value, sometimes manifold, without either effort or contribution on his part; and that is justice!"

According to Guy Shrubsole in his excellent polemic *Who Owns England?* (2019), in the still-incomplete figures obtained from the Land Registry, the aristocracy and landed gentry still own an astonishing 30 per cent of England; so-called "new money" (e.g. industrialists, Russian oligarchs and bankers), 17 per cent; and the public sector, 8.5 per cent. Only 2 per cent is owned by conservation charities such as the National Trust, the RSPB and the Woodland Trust and just 5 per cent by ordinary homeowners. Amazingly, 17 per cent of the land in England and Wales remains unregistered, its ownership unknown.

The inequality of landownership in England is brought into even greater relief when the figures for farmland ownership is taken into consideration, according to Shrubsole. He estimates that 25,000 landowners – less than 1 per cent of the population – own half of England.

Shrubsole claims that little has actually changed since the days of Domesday. "At the time of the Domesday Book in 1086, some 200 Norman barons owned half of England. Thanks to the miracle of trickle-down economics, that elite expanded over time – so that a mere eight centuries later, half of England lay in the hands of 4,000 aristocrats and members of the gentry."

On the twentieth anniversary of the Countryside and Rights of Way Act, which admittedly gave us only partial access to our open countryside, great encouragement can be gained from the way in which the legislation has been accepted and has worked on the ground. The initial, frankly scaremongering, fears which landowners expressed of an enormous rural crime wave, vandalism and fires on the passing of CRoW have all been proved to be totally unfounded.

And the setting-up of Local Access Forums, on which landowners, conservation bodies and all types of recreational users, from horse riders to mountain bikers, sit round the table to discuss and resolve where possible matters of mutual concern, has proved to be one of the best things to come from the CRoW Act. Something to crow about, in fact.

But there is no doubt that threats remain. The Conservative election manifesto of 2019 pledged to "criminalise unintentional trespass", which could see yet another attempt to make trespass a criminal offence, something that was first suggested over eighty years ago in the hated Access to Mountains Act of 1939. The Ramblers are calling on the government to rethink its plans to change trespass laws, amid concerns that the moves could have the consequence of eroding walkers' rights and deterring people from walking in or just visiting the countryside.

Theoretically, the recent Home Office consultation is about strengthening police powers to tackle unauthorised encampments by travellers. But there is a serious lack of clarity in the consultation document. Without a clear definition of "residing", for example, there is a risk to the right to protest in the countryside, for example against unwanted and damaging developments such as road schemes, and to the innocent pleasure of "wild" camping. Trespass is currently a civil wrong and criminalisation would constitute a major change in the law – and one that could have a significant impact on walkers.

Gemma Cantelo, the Ramblers' Head of Policy and Advocacy, commented:

> We're worried that these proposals are the thin edge of a wedge which could result in an erosion of people's rights to access and enjoy the countryside. It's vital that the access rights that the Ramblers and others have fought for over the years are protected. A reported 84 per cent of police forces do not support the criminalisation of unauthorised encampments, so this seems like a sledgehammer approach to policymaking.

The Government's priority should be to make it easier for people to get outside and enjoy the benefits of walking and nature. It's been proved that they are good both for our health and for the planet.

Cantelo added: "It's critical that these proposals do not have a detrimental impact for walkers – and the Ramblers are raising these concerns with the Government."

The Ramblers says it exists to protect people's ability to enjoy the benefits and sense of freedom that come from being outdoors on foot, and it opposes any measures that would deter people from exercising their rights to access the outdoors. At the moment, walkers may have to leave a footpath to get past an obstruction, they may stray from the right of way by accident, or they may have sincerely held beliefs that they have a right of way. The mere act of walking in the countryside should not put anyone at risk of committing a crime, it insists.

Current Ramblers' chair Kate Ashbrook (see Chapter 18) confirms: "Our work is far from finished. We still have a long way to go in England and Wales. All open country should be included in access land. And what about woodlands and riverbanks, which also provide magnificent opportunities for walkers? There is still much to campaign for but, 20 years on, let's celebrate the access we have won – our right to wander freely from the path over acres of glorious countryside."

I can do no better than conclude with the sentiments expressed in the last verse and chorus of Ewan MacColl's "The Manchester Rambler", a verse of which started this book. Purists will note that the words in the last line of the chorus have been slightly changed from "I am a free man" to "I have my freedom." There's a story attached to this. I had invited MacColl's former wife Peggy Seeger, sister of US folk legend Pete Seeger, to sing the song after Trespass leader Benny Rothman had unveiled a copy of the plaque celebrating the Mass Trespass at Bowden Bridge, Hayfield at the Edale Information Centre in 1991. But as an ardent feminist, she refused to sing the words "free man."

"But that's what Ewan wrote," I protested.

"But that's not what he meant," she replied.

So this is what she sang, and what we always lustily sing today at the conclusion of our annual Spirit of Kinder celebrations:

*So I'll walk where I will over mountain and hill*
*And I'll lie where the bracken is deep;*
*I belong to the mountains, the clear running fountains*
*Where the grey rocks rise rugged and steep.*
*I've seen the white hare in the gulleys,*
*And the curlew fly high overhead,*
*And sooner than part from the mountains*
*I think I would rather be dead.*
　　*Chorus*
　　*I'm a rambler, I'm a rambler from Manchester way*
　　*I get all my pleasure the hard moorland way;*
　　*I may be a wage slave on Monday*
　　*But I have my freedom on Sunday.*

# Further Reading

Bainbridge, John, *The Compleat Trespasser*, Fellside Books (2014)
    *Wayfarer's Dole*, Fellside Books (2016)
Bate, Jonathan, *John Clare: a Biography*, Picador (2003)
Blunden, John and Curry, Michael (eds.), *A People's Charter?* Countryside Commission (1990)
Clayton, Peter, *Octavia Hill*, Pitkin Guides (2012)
Fox, Stephen, *John Muir and his Legacy: The American Conservation Movement*, Little, Brown & Company (1981)
Gallimore, Ethel Bassett, *The Pride of the Peak*, Jonathan Cape (1926)
Garside, Luke, *Kinder Scout: The footpaths and bridle-roads about Hayfield etc*, Willow Publishing (1880, reprint 1980)
Graham, Stephen, *The Gentle Art of Tramping*, Robert Holding (1926), reprinted by Bloomsbury Reader (2019)
Hayes, Nick, *The Book of Trespass*, Bloomsbury (2020)
Hill, Howard, *Freedom to Roam: The Struggle for Access to Britain's Moors and Mountains*, Moorland Publishing (1980)
Jones, Melvyn, *Protecting the Beautiful Frame*, Sheffield and Peak branch of CPRE (2001)
Legg, Rodney, *Steep Holm: Allsop Island*, Wincanton Press (1992)
    *Legg over Dorset*, Halsgrove Publishing (2011)
MacColl, Ewan, *Journeyman: An Autobiography*, Sidgwick & Jackson (1990)
McOwan, Rennie, *The Man Who Bought Mountains*, National Trust for Scotland (1977)
Monkhouse, Patrick, *On Foot in the Peak*, Alexander Maclehose (1932)
Moyse, Peter, *John Clare: The Poet and the Place*, John Clare Society (1999)
Muir, John, *The Story of my Boyhood and Youth*, Sierra Club (1988)
    *The Yosemite*, Sierra Club (1988)
Perrin, Jim, *On and Off the Rocks*, Victor Gollancz (1986)
    *Yes, to Dance: Essays From Outside the Stockade*, Oxford Illustrated Press (1990)
    *Travels with the Flea*, In Pinn (2002)
    *West: A Journey through the Landscapes of Loss*, Atlantic Books (2010)

Reynolds, Fiona, *The Fight for Beauty*, Oneworld Publications (2016)

Rothman, Benny, *The Battle for Kinder Scout*, Willow Publishing (1982 and 2012)

Sayer, Sylvia, *Wild Country*, Dartmoor Preservation Association (2000)

Shoard, Marion, *The Theft of the Countryside*, Maurice Temple Smith (1980)
> *This Land is our Land*, Paladin Books (1987)
> *A Right to Roam*, Oxford University Press (1999)

Shrubsole, Guy, *Who Owns England?* William Collins (2019)

Sissons, David (ed.), *The Best of the Clarion Ramblers' Handbooks*, Halsgrove Publishing (2002)

Sissons, Dave, Howard, Terry and Smith, Roly, *Right to Roam: A Celebration of the Sheffield Campaign for Access to Moorland*, Northend Creative Print/SCAM (2005)
> *Clarion Call: Sheffield's Access Pioneers*, Northend Creative Print (2017)

Smith, Roly, *First and Last*, Peak Park Joint Planning Board (1978)
> *Peak National Park*, Webb & Bower (1987)
> *The Peak District, Official National Park Guide* Pevensey Guides (2000)
> (ed.), *Kinder Scout: Portrait of a Mountain*, Derbyshire County Council (2002)
> *The Pennine Way*, Frances Lincoln (2011)

Speakman, Colin, *The Dales Way*, Dalesman Publishing (1970)
> *Yorkshire Dales: Official National Park Guide*, Pevensey Guides (2001)
> *Walk! A celebration of stepping out*, Great Northern Books (2011)
> *The Yorkshire Dales National Park: A Celebration of 60 Years,* Great Northern Books (2014)
> with Tony Grogan, *50 Years of the Dales Way*, Skyware (2019)

Stephenson, Tom, *Forbidden Land: The Struggle for Access to Mountain and Moorland*, Manchester University Press (1989)

Ward, GHB, *Sheffield Clarion Ramblers' Handbooks*, (1912-1958)

Wilkinson, David, *Fight for It Now: John Dower and the Struggle for National Parks in Britain*, Signal Books (2019)

Worster, Donald, *A Passion for Nature: The Life of John Muir*, Oxford University Press (2008)

# Acknowledgements

THE IDEA FOR THIS BOOK arose from two series of features the author wrote about some of these characters which were originally published in *The Great Outdoors* (*TGO*) and *BBC Countryfile* magazines. I am indebted to their respective editors, Carey Davies and Fergus Collins, for kindly permitting me to expand the idea into this book.

The publisher and I are also grateful to Tom Platt, Director of Advocacy and Engagement at the Ramblers, for his generous support of the book.

Without exception, I received the most generous and gracious help and support from all the living subjects featured in this book. Many said they were honoured to be included, and I must say I am equally honoured that they agreed to be featured, and to count them as among the best of my friends.

In addition, Agnes McOwan and her daughter Lesley Andrews were generous in their help about Rennie and Percy Unna, as was Prof Harry Rothman on the chapter on his father Benny, while Dave Sissons kindly checked my facts about Bert Ward. Denise Lyons of Halsgrove Publishing was also helpful in providing information about Rodney Legg.

The lyrics of "The Manchester Rambler" are reprinted with permission from *The Essential Ewan MacColl Songbook* (Oak Publications, 2001).

Finally a special word of thanks must go to Ramblers' president, radio DJ, TV presenter, author and journalist Stuart Maconie, who has been a long-time supporter of our annual Spirit of Kinder events, for his generous foreword.

# Feel inspired?

**Discover the joy of walking…**
**Join the Ramblers today**

Join the largest walking community in Great Britain, and you'll enjoy access to hundreds of free group walks, whilst protecting the walking environments you love.

Become a member and you'll enjoy:

- Unlimited free access to hundreds of group walks every week
- A searchable library of routes on our website and app for you to discover new walks every day
- Four issues of Walk magazine a year packed full of kit reviews, life-changing stories and great routes
- Special member offers including 15% off Cotswold Outdoor

Fall in love with the great outdoors, make new friends and protect the places we all love to *walk*.

Join at ramblers.org.uk/join, or call 020 3961 3232 (Monday to Friday 9am-5pm).

**ramblers**
at the heart of walking

## Also from Signal Books

www.signalbooks.co.uk

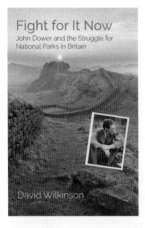

**Fight for It Now**
**David Wilkinson**
**£25.00 hb**
**ISBN: 9781909930797**

National Parks are Britain's breathing spaces – protected areas enjoyed by the millions of visitors attracted every year by their tranquillity, beauty and landscape. Fifteen National Parks cover a significant share of Britain's total land area – 10 per cent of England, 20 per cent of Wales, and 7 per cent of Scotland. Yet despite their importance, few people today are aware of the campaign in the 1930s and 1940s to establish National Parks. And fewer still know the name of the man who was its principal driving force.

John Dower was an architect, a planner, a prodigious walker, an accomplished writer and, above all, a fighter. *Fight for It Now* is the first biography to be written about him, and the title reflects his one great objective and the increasing urgency of attaining it as his health declined. Drawing on extensive national archives and his private papers and letters, the book describes Dower's early work with pressure groups like the Friends of the Lake District and the Council for the Protection of Rural England, and then his subsequent move during the Second World War to an influential position inside government, focusing on post-war reconstruction. While German bombs were falling on British cities, it was part of Dower's job to quarter the English countryside and identify potential areas for National Parks.

Dower's most influential contribution was his 'one-man White Paper' *National Parks in England and Wales* published at the end of the war in 1945. The 'Dower Report' addressed key questions on the criteria for selecting National Parks, where they should be located, who they were for, and how they should be administered, and it paved the way at last for the 1949 National Parks and Access to the Countryside Act, seventy years ago this year. While overcoming opponents both outside and inside government, Dower wrote continuously as though his project could only be hammered out at white heat. And all the while, the one struggle he knew he could not win was the tuberculosis that eventually killed him, at the tragically early age of forty-seven.

For most of his working life, David Wilkinson has researched and lectured on British and European environmental policy and politics – within higher education, an environmental think-tank, and the UK's wildlife and countryside agency, Natural England. *Fight for it Now* is the second of his biographies of pioneer environmental campaigners, and follows a portrait of writer and broadcaster, Kenneth Allsop (*Keeping the Barbarians* at Bay, Signal Books 2013).